WJEC B Religious Studies
Religion & Life Issues

Helen Bartley • Laura Burridge
Tanya Hill • Chris Owens

Series Editor: Chris Owens

WJEC
CBAC

Helping every student get better grades

Heinemann is an imprint of Pearson Education Limited, a company incorporated in England and Wales, having its registered office at Edinburgh Gate, Harlow, Essex, CM20 2JE. Registered company number: 872828

www.heinemann.co.uk

Heinemann is a registered trademark of Pearson Education Limited

Text © Helen Bartley, Laura Burridge, Tanya Hill and Chris Owens 2009

First published 2009

13 12 11 10 09
10 9 8 7 6 5 4 3 2

British Library Cataloguing in Publication Data
A catalogue record for this book is available from the British Library

ISBN 978 0 435501 61 7

Edited by Florence Production Ltd, Stoodleigh, Devon
Reviewed by Graham Davies
Designed by Wooden Ark Studios
Typeset by 🅣 Tek-Art, Crawley Down, West Sussex
Produced by Florence Production Ltd, Stoodleigh, Devon
Original illustrations © Pearson Education Ltd
Illustrated by Ben Swift
Cover design by Pearson Education Ltd
Picture research by Susi Paz
Cover photo/illustration © Chris Parker
Printed in China (SWTC/02)

The author and publisher would like to thank the following individuals and organisations for permission to reproduce photographs:

© Alamy/Alex Segre p. 59; © Alamy/Andrew Paterson p. 112; © Alamy/Blend Images p. 34; © Alamy/Brad Cherson p. 97; © Alamy/Chris Fredriksson p. 78; © Alamy/ClassicStock p. 39; © Alamy/Eagle Visions Photography/Craig Lovell p. 85; © Alamy/Graham Bell p. 97; © Alamy/Ian Miles-Flashpoint Pictures p. 84; © Alamy/Israel Images p. 112; © Alamy/Janine Wiedel Photolibrary p. 56; © Alamy/Mario Ponta p. 47; © Alamy/Motoring Picture Library p. 82; © Alamy/The Natural History Museum p. 93; © Alamy/Peter Barritt pp. 24, 112; © Alamy/Photos 12 p. 76; © Alamy/Robert Fried p. 46; © Alamy/Rubber Ball p. 16; © Alamy/Sally and Richard Greenhill p. 82; © Alamy/Steve Allen Travel Photography p. 34; © Alamy/World Religions Photo Library p. 18; © Corbis/Immaginazione/Gianni Giansanti p. 34; © Getty Images/AFP/Roberto Schmidt p. 52; © Getty Images/Robert Harding World Imagery/Jochen Schenkler p. 80; © Getty Images/Stone/Adrian Neal p. 78; © Getty Images/Time & Life Pictures/William F. Campbell p. 59; © iStockPhotos/Curt Pickens p. 18; © iStockPhotos/Erick Jones p. 28; © iStockPhotos/Geoffrey Holman p. 71; © iStockPhotos/James Richey p. 106; © iStockPhotos/Justin Horrocks p. 106; © iStockPhotos/Luoman p. 110; © iStockPhotos/René Mansi p. 70; © iStockPhotos/Sandra O'Claire p. 32; © iStockPhotos/Tobias Helbig p. 108; © iStockPhotos/TommL p. 13; © Muslim Aid p. 50; © NASA p. 65; © PA Photos/AP/Charles Dharapak p. 59; © PA Photos/AP/Hasan Sarbakhshian p. 34; © PA Photos/PA Archive/Yui Mok p. 55; © PhotoDisc/StockTrek pp. 91, 112; © Procuraduria General de la Republica p. 48; © ROKPA p. 50

All Bible verses are taken from the **New Revised Standard Version Bible**, copyright © 1989 National Council of the Churches of Christ in the United States of America. Used by permission. All rights reserved. All verses from the Qur'an are used with permission of IPCI – Islamic Vision, Birmingham, UK.

p. 46 statistics from Central Intelligence Agency; p. 65 "ONE OF US" Words and music by ERIC BAZILIAN © 1995 HUMAN BOY MUSIC. All rights administered by WB MUSIC CORP. All rights reserved. Used by permission from ALFRED PUBLISHING CO., INC; p. 80 Mary Elizabeth Fry; p. 91 "EARTH SONG" Words and music by MICHAEL JACKSON © 1995 MIJAC MUSIC. All rights administered by WARNER-TAMERLANE PUBLISHING CORP. All rights reserved. Used by permission from ALFRED PUBLISHING CO., INC; p. 99 Joyce C. Lock © 2002.

Every effort has been made to contact copyright holders of material reproduced in this book. Any omissions will be rectified in subsequent printings if notice is given to the publishers.

Contents

Introduction

A note for teachers

This student book has been written especially to support the WJEC Religious Studies Specification B, Unit 1: *Religion and life issues* (full and short course). It covers the six principal religions of the specification (Buddhism, Christianity, Hinduism, Islam, Judaism and Sikhism) and is part of an overall series comprising:

- a second student book covering Unit 2 of the specification (*Religion and human experience*)
- a Teacher Guide covering both units, and
- an Active Teach CD-ROM containing support materials for both students and teachers.

The specification provides an ideal opportunity to gain a qualification in Religious Studies while studying a thematic course that looks in detail at some of the fascinating central questions and issues in human life and experience. The material covers the relevance of religious beliefs, practices, values and traditions related to these questions.

This book has been carefully based on the WJEC specification content, and develops approaches to learning and teaching that promote both engagement and enjoyment with challenge and support.

The authors

The authors of this student book are all teachers in England and Wales as well as being WJEC examiners. This means that they understand the demands of the specification and have therefore sensitively compiled a book to meet the requirements of students taking the course.

With the development of a new specification came the distinct need for a student book to explain the significant changes and provide a coherent and structured guide to the course. The result is this student book, which offers a comprehensive structure to following the course as well as providing information, lesson ideas and activities along with clear teaching and learning objectives for all teachers (including non-specialists).

Usefully, this book can also be used by students following GCSE Religious Studies courses on other boards, although students should check their course specifications with their teacher.

Purpose of the specification

WJEC Religious Studies Specification B, Unit 1: *Religion and life issues* offers a contemporary approach to the study of religious education. It is different and distinct from many other examination board specifications, as it supports the use of a full page of visual stimuli for each question in the examination. The rationale here is that this helps students to identify with the issues involved and encourages them to be inspired, moved and changed by following a broad, satisfying and worthwhile course of study that challenges them and equips them to lead constructive lives in the modern world. The promotion of community cohesion is at the heart of this course.

Why a new book?

Changes to the specification

The specification has changed according to the changing nature of education and the need to meet the demands of the world for students. The main changes that teachers and students should be aware of include the following:

- There has been a reduction in the number of topics to four (Topic 1: Relationships; Topic 2: Is it fair?; Topic 3: Looking for meaning; Topic 4: Our world), along with a change of content in those topics. The reduction is the result of new assessment objectives (AOs).
- There is a 50 per cent focus now given to AO1 (Describe, explain and analyse, using knowledge and understanding) and a 50 per cent focus to AO2 (Use evidence and reasoned argument to express and evaluate personal responses, informed insights and differing viewpoints). Previously the focus was 75% on AO1 and 25% on AO2. There is more information on this on pages 9–11.

- There have been changes to the key concepts and key words in each topic.
- Level descriptor grids have been changed to a new range of 0 to 8 marks for extended questions.
- QWC (Quality of Written Communication) is now only assessed on the extended writing sections.
- There have been changes to the style of the questions on the examination paper – for example, the 'state' questions have been removed and more emphasis has been given to extended writing answers (with more space for answers dedicated to these on the examination paper).
- There is an increased focus on learning *from* religion rather than simply learning *about* religion, and explicit reference to religious beliefs is now required in all extended writing answers. Students are now expected to refer to Christianity and no more than two other religious traditions in their answers on the examination paper.
- 'Religious believers' is the new term used in examination questions when focusing on religious ideas.

Notes for teachers and students

Aims of this book

From the beginning to the end, this book provides a relevant, practical and comprehensive guide to this course. It supports both teachers and students in their study of the four topics from the initial viewing of the material through to revision and the examination. This resource allows students to develop their knowledge and understanding of the religions studied. It also gives them the opportunity to consider many current and important issues from religious and non-religious perspectives.

Skills are a vital element in any GCSE course, and this book will provide invaluable assistance to students in:

- developing skills when considering religious and other responses to moral, ethical and philosophical issues
- identifying, investigating and responding to fundamental questions of life and living.

Examination focus of the book

This book provides an all-important focus on the examination techniques required to pass the GCSE in Religious Studies. It gives advice on general revision and, more specifically, how to prepare successfully and get through the examination. After all, this is the ultimate outcome of the specification.

The **Grade Studio** features that appear throughout, and at the end of, each topic (see page 7 for more details) give students a thorough knowledge of the level descriptors used by examiners to mark their responses. They also allow an important insight into how to improve weaker answers and secure higher marks.

The **Exam Café** feature on pages 116–123 carefully takes each student, step by step, through a preparation route to sitting their exams. In an easily digestible format, it offers practical, yet realistic, advice and guidance about revising and achieving the optimum grade.

Religion and life issues has been specifically written to provide comprehensive coverage of the key ideas and issues involved in the specification. It is designed to:

- be informative yet accessible to all students, and
- provide invaluable support throughout the course study.

What's in this book

This student book, which works in conjunction with the WJEC Religious Studies Specification B, Unit 1: *Religion and life issues*, has the following sections:

- the **introduction**, which you are reading now
- the **four topics** covered in the specification (Topic 1: Relationships; Topic 2: Is it fair?; Topic 3: Looking for meaning; Topic 4: Our world)
- **Exam Café** – an invaluable resource for students studying for their GCSE in Religious Studies
- **Glossary** – a reference tool for key terms and words used throughout the book.
- **Active Book CD-ROM** – an electronic version of the book on a CD in the back of every copy of the book; the CD also contains an interactive Exam Café.

The four topics

Each topic contains:

- a topic scene-setter (**The Big Picture**)
- a look at the key questions raised by the topic, and the key words and issues associated with those questions (**Develop Your Knowledge**)
- nine two-page spreads covering the **main topic content**
- two pages of different level questions to check understanding of the topic material (**Remember and Reflect**)
- exam-style questions with level indicators, examiner's comments and model answers (**Grade Studio**).

These features, which are explained more fully in the following pages, have been carefully planned and designed to draw together the WJEC specification in a manageable and convenient way.

The Big Picture

This provides an overview of the topic. It explains to students what they will be studying (the content), why they are studying it (the relevance) and how they will study it (the approaches, activities and tasks). It also includes a 'Get started' activity, often linked to a picture or visual stimulus, which presents a task designed to engage students in the issues of the topic and give them some idea of the content to be studied.

Develop Your Knowledge

This lists the key information, key words and key questions of the topic. At a glance, it allows students to grasp the basic elements of knowledge they will gain in the study of the topic. It is also a useful reference point for reflection and checking information as it is studied.

Main topic content

The main content of each topic is covered in nine two-page spreads. Each spread equates to roughly one lesson of work – although teachers will need to judge for themselves if some of these will need more time.

Each spread begins with the learning outcomes, so that students are aware of the focus and aims of the lesson. It then poses a leading question, often in connection with a visual stimulus, which encourages students to think quickly in general terms about the specific issues they will cover.

The text then attempts to answer, through a balanced viewpoint, one or two of the key questions raised in **Develop Your Knowledge**. The text carefully covers the views of both religious believers and non-believers. It is also punctuated with activities that range from simple tasks that can take place in the classroom to more complex tasks that can be tackled away from school.

A range of margin features adds extra depth and support to the main text for both students and the teacher:

- 'For debate' invites students to examine two sides of a controversial issue.
- 'Must think about!' directs students towards a key idea that they should consider.
- 'Sacred text' provides an extract from one of the religions covered in the topic to help students understand religious ideas and teachings.
- 'Research note' provides specific guidance about how students can research for themselves a particular issue/person/idea or event.

Remember and Reflect

This provides an opportunity for students to reflect on what they have learned and identify possible weaknesses or gaps in their knowledge. It also helps them to recognise key ideas in the specification content. Once students have tested their knowledge with the first set of questions, a cross-reference takes them back to the relevant part of the text so they can check their answers. A second set of questions helps them to develop the skills necessary for the examination.

Grade Studio

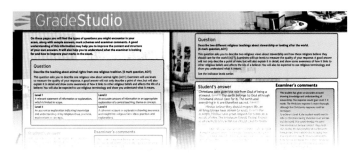

This exciting and integral feature allows students to gain a valuable understanding of what examiners are looking for. It is available as part of each topic in the student book and also as an interactive feature.

Grade Studio features in two ways throughout each topic:

- it appears in boxes through the main spreads as an extra consideration in relation to the lesson studied, and
- it appears as a two-page spread at the end of each topic with a range of different-level student answers and examiner responses.

It helps students to become familiar with the level descriptors for both assessment objectives 1 and 2 (AO1 and AO2), and provides an explicit focus on how students can improve their answers using building skills and techniques. It has practice questions built in to give students some idea about the style of examination questions and how to provide high-level answers in response to them. (More information on the level descriptors and AO1/AO2 grids can be found on pages 9–11.)

Exam Café

This feature has been specially designed to support students as they prepare for and approach the examination. It provides realistic and practical guidance on how to plan revision effectively and monitor knowledge and understanding of each topic. Exam Café contains:

- useful and practical revision tips for students
- comments from an examiner on how a student's overall performance can be improved
- a checklist for studying each topic
- tasks that test revision strategies.

It is a motivating feature carefully put together to help engage students in effective revision, an aspect of the course that many students find difficult. As well as being an integral part of the student book, this feature is also available on the accompanying Active Teach CD-ROM.

Other resources in the series

Teacher Guide

This guide essentially provides teachers with suggestions for teaching the whole of WJEC Religious Studies Specification B – Units 1 and 2.

Each topic in this guide contains ten spread-based lesson plans (one for **The Big Picture**, plus a further nine to correspond with the main content spreads in each student book). These plans give an exciting and engaging range of ideas and material that teachers can draw on to teach alongside or to supplement the content of the student book. In addition, each lesson plan comes with either a supporting photocopiable worksheet or background notes on the three religions *not* covered in each topic.

Each lesson plan in the guide is meticulously cross-referenced to the corresponding materials in both student books. It also contains the lesson focus and learning outcomes as stated in the student books, then moves through a series of starter activities, development ideas, plenaries and homework/extension tasks. These have all been written to cover the student book lessons from as many angles as possible, to help students think all the way round what are often sensitive and difficult issues that may well be outside their range of experience at this point in their lives.

The activities, discussions, ideas and debates have all been designed and road-tested to inspire and motivate students to learn as thoroughly as possible the content of the specification.

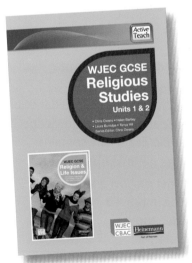

Active Teach CD-ROM

This is designed to support the materials in both student books and the Teacher Guide. It is an exciting set of resources that will help to make lesson activities more interactive. These activities work best with an interactive whiteboard, but could also be used individually on computers. The interactives include specially designed Grade Studio activities, which complement and extend the Grade Studio in this book. The Active Teach CD-ROM also contains extra worksheets and pictures that can be used in the delivery of the course.

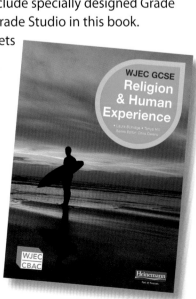

Student book 2 – Religion & Human Experience

The second student book accompanying the WJEC course Specification B, Unit 2 takes a similar format to this student book but focuses on four different topics:

- Topic 1 Religion and conflict
- Topic 2 Religion and medicine
- Topic 3 Religious expression
- Topic 4 Authority: Religion and the state.

About the exam

The WJEC GCSE Religious Studies Specification B, Unit 1 option is assessed by a written paper of 1 hour 45 minutes. This paper contains four main sections – one for each topic studied. Each section comprises five parts, labelled **a–e**.

Students are required to answer all the questions on the paper. Writing lines are provided for them to write their responses, giving them some guidance on the expected length of their answers. The number of marks available for each question is clearly shown, and all questions follow a set format and style. Students' answers are marked using level descriptor grids (which can be found on pages 10–11). They are assessed according to the following objectives.

■ AO1: Describe, explain and analyse, using knowledge and understanding.
■ AO2: Use evidence and reasoned argument to express and evaluate personal responses, informed insights and differing viewpoints.

AO1 and AO2 are weighted equally in the paper (50 per cent each) and are interrelated, which means students should show connections between ideas. Students need to be made aware of the differences in AO1 and AO2 and the style of questions in the examination in order to succeed in this paper.

The information that follows outlines the set structure of the questions, including the numbers of marks available and the focus of assessment for each question.

a These questions are always worth 2 marks; they use AO1 assessment, and the corresponding level grid descriptors are used to mark this type of response. These questions focus on key concepts. They look at what religious believers mean by using particular terms in relation to one of the key ideas within each topic of study – for example: *Explain what religious believers mean by the term _____.*

b These questions are always worth 4 marks; they use AO1 assessment, and the corresponding level grid descriptors are used to mark this type of response. The focus is on students showing their knowledge and understanding of how the beliefs of religious believers mean that they act or view something in a particular way – for example: *Explain how having a religious faith may _____.*

c These questions are always worth 4 marks; they use AO2 assessment, and the corresponding level grid descriptors are used to mark this type of response. The focus is on students explaining why a religious believer would agree or disagree with a given statement of information – for example: *'Statement.' Give two reasons why a religious believer might agree or disagree with this statement.*

d These questions are always worth 6 marks; they use AO1 assessment, and the corresponding level grid descriptors are used to mark this type of response. The focus is on students showing knowledge and understanding about the practices and teachings of key religions. Detail and explanation are required in their answers rather than simply description – for example: *Explain from two different religious traditions the teachings about _____.*

e These questions are always worth 8 marks; they use AO2 assessment, and the corresponding level grid descriptors are used to mark this type of response. The focus is on students giving their own views about some of the issues studied, as well as showing their awareness of a range of other views and drawing on religious and moral knowledge to show the impact issues might have on individuals and society. The question always begins with a statement, which is the focus of the answer – for example: *'Statement.' Do you agree? Give reasons or evidence for your answer, showing that you have thought of more than one point of view. You must include reference to religious beliefs in your answer.*

Marking grids and level descriptors

AO1

The level grid descriptors show the development of answers up the scale. AO1 focuses on knowledge and understanding; the higher levels indicate that students need to be able to relate ideas together and be concise, detailed and thorough in their answers. There are four levels for each descriptor (apart from the 2 mark questions), and please note that the higher levels in the 6 mark questions have more than 1 mark available.

2 mark questions (question a)

Level	Level descriptor	Mark total
0	No statement of relevant information or explanation.	0
1	A statement of information or explanation which is limited in scope or content.	1
2	An accurate and appropriate explanation of a central teaching, theme or concept.	2

4 mark questions (question b)

Level	Level descriptor	Mark total
0	Makes no link between beliefs and practices.	0
1	A simple link between beliefs and practices.	1
2	An explicit link between beliefs and practices. Limited use of specialist language.	2
3	Analysis showing some awareness and insight into religious facts, ideas, practices and explanations. Uses and interprets a range of religious language and terms.	3
4	Coherent analysis showing awareness and insight into religious facts, ideas, practices and explanations. Uses religious language and terms extensively and interprets them accurately.	4

6 mark questions (question d)

Level	Level descriptor	Mark total
0	A statement of information or explanation, which has no relevant content.	0
1	A relevant statement of information or explanation, which is limited in scope.	1
2	An accurate account of information or an appropriate explanation of a central teaching, theme or concept. Limited use of religious language.	2
3	An account or explanation indicating knowledge and understanding of key religious ideas, practices, explanations or concepts. Uses and interprets religious language in appropriate context.	3–4
4	A coherent account or explanation showing awareness and insight into religious facts, ideas, practices and explanations. Uses religious language and terms extensively and interprets them accurately.	5–6

AO2

The level descriptors show the development of answers up the scale. AO2 focuses on students explaining the reasoning behind different views and, more importantly, justifying their own opinions. The higher levels indicate that students need to be able to relate ideas together and be concise, detailed and thorough in their answers. There are four levels for each descriptor, and please note that the higher levels in the 8 mark questions have more than 1 mark available.

4 mark questions (question c)

Level	Level descriptor	Mark total
0	Makes no relevant point of view.	0
1	A simple, appropriate justification of a point of view.	1
2	EITHER an expanded justification of one point of view, with appropriate example and /or illustration, which includes religious teaching OR two simple, appropriate justifications of a point of view.	2
3	An expanded justification of one point of view, with appropriate example and/or illustration, which includes religious teaching with a second simple appropriate justification of a point of view (which may be an alternative to the first).	3
4	An expanded justification of two viewpoints, incorporating the religious teaching and moral aspects at issue and their implications for the individual and the rest of society.	4

8 mark questions (question e)

Level	Level descriptor	Mark total
0	Makes no relevant point of view.	0
1	Communicates clearly and appropriately EITHER a simple, justification of a point of view, possibly linked to evidence or example and making a simple connection between religion and people's lives OR two simple appropriate justifications of points of view.	1–2
2	Communicates clearly and appropriately, using limited specialist language, EITHER an expanded justification of one point of view, with appropriate example, which includes religious teaching and /or illustration AND either a second simple appropriate justification OR two, appropriate justifications of points of view linked to evidence or example, which includes religious teaching.	3–4
3	Communicates clearly and appropriately, using and interpreting specialist language, an expanded justification of one point of view, with appropriate examples, which include religious teaching and/or illustration. There is also an adequate recognition of an alternative or different point of view.	5–6
4	Communicates clearly and appropriately, using specialist language extensively, a thorough discussion, including alternative or different views of the religious teachings and moral aspects at issue and their implications for the individual and the rest of society. Uses relevant evidence and religious/or moral reasoning to formulate judgement.	7–8

1 Relationships

The Big Picture

- In this topic you will be addressing religious issues about relationships
- This topic covers three principal religions: Christianity, Judaism and Sikhism
- You will need to focus on at least two principal religions.

You will look at:

- issues of love, marriage and divorce
- Christian ideas about love
- the commitments and responsibilities we have towards each other
- religious teachings on:
  - adultery, divorce and remarriage, and the role and purpose of sex
  - courtship, the meaning of marriage and wedding ceremonies, and remarriage
  - same-sex relationships.

You will also think about the ways in which these beliefs affect all the issues connected with love, marriage and divorce.

What?

You will:

- learn about religious beliefs, practices, values and traditions
- look at human experiences and issues
- study six key concepts.

Why?

Because:

- this will help you to explore your own beliefs, and develop a sense of identity and belonging
- recognising and valuing the religious beliefs of others can help you to understand why religious believers think and act in the ways they do
- considering the moral values and attitudes of individuals, faith communities or contemporary society helps you to understand what others believe and allows you to explore your own opinions.

How?

By:

- studying and recalling the teaching of three world religions on these issues
- thinking about the relevance and practical application of these teachings in today's world
- analysing the views of religious believers and comparing them to your own views.

Get started

Imagine you have been invited to a television debate (such as the BBC programme *Question Time*). The theme is church wedding ceremonies, and the two opposing viewpoints are as follows.

Viewpoint 1

> *You should only get married in church if you believe in God.*

Viewpoint 2

> *If you want a big fancy wedding in church, it doesn't matter if you don't believe in God.*

1   List three things you think would support each viewpoint.

2   In pairs, compare the points you have made for each viewpoint. Are you able to agree on a list of three points for each viewpoint?

3   As a class, list the main issues raised about marrying in a church. In general, which viewpoint does the class support?

Develop Your Knowledge

This topic is about the issues of love, marriage and divorce. Read the information below, which will help you to think about all aspects of relationships before you begin more detailed work.

Key information

- There are different kinds of love, including the concept of unconditional or unselfish love, within the Christian tradition.

- In today's world there are many different types of relationships. Marriage is just one of them.

- Family life within religious traditions comes with commitment, roles and responsibilities.

- Marriage ceremonies from different religions vary because of the different beliefs of the religions.

- Adultery (where someone who is still married has a sexual relationship with someone else) is regarded as wrong.

- Conflict is part of human relationships, as is reconciliation. Some people turn to religious beliefs and teachings for help.

- Living together and same-sex relationships are familiar aspects of modern life in some societies.

- Modern ways of living may be responsible for changing people's perceptions of the importance and value of marriage.

- Different religions have different viewpoints on divorce.

- Divorced people may find it hard to remarry in a religious ceremony.

Key words

celibacy abstinence from a sexual relationship

chastity no sex before marriage; to remain sexually pure for marriage

commitment sense of dedication and obligation to someone or something

conflict stresses and strains that take place within all human relationships

love one of the most powerful human emotions, which joins people together

reconciliation saying sorry and making up after an argument

relationship an emotional association between two people

responsibilities actions you are expected to carry out

rite of passage something that marks a change in a person's status and an important stage in life

sacrament an outward sign of an inward change that involves God's blessing

tradition belief, custom or common practice

vow promise between people, or between a person and God

- What is love?
- What commitments do we have to others?
- What responsibilities do we have towards each other?
- What is the role and purpose of sex?
- Whose decision is it concerning the use of contraception?
- Is marriage out of date?
- How important is the family?
- Is it necessary to marry in a place of worship?
- Why do some marriages succeed and others fail?
- Should people be allowed to remarry?
- Should remarriage take place in a religious building?
- Should same-sex marriage be allowed in a place of worship?

For interest

Think about why human beings have relationships. Then imagine you have to spend the rest of your life on a desert island. You can choose nine other people to live with you on the island. You will have some sort of relationship with each of these people. Who would you choose and why? You must be able to give one or more reasons for choosing each person.

Think ten years ahead, to when you are about 26 years old. What people might you develop relationships with between now and then?

Now imagine you are unmarried at that point in your life and you want to find a suitable partner to marry. If you had to describe yourself, what would you write? You have a maximum of 50 words. (A photograph will accompany your text, so you should not give a physical description.) If you need help with your description of yourself, ask a friend to help you.

What kind of person do you think would suit you? In no more than 100 words, write your description.

1.1 Relationships and love (1)

The next two pages will help you to:

■ explore the different relationships people have with each other
■ identify the different types of love they may encounter.

■ **What do you think 'relationship' means?**

■ **How many people do you think you have a relationship with?**

What is love?

How human beings relate to each other is one of the fundamental building blocks of society. Religion is all about how humans relate to **God** and to each other. In the **Christian** religion Jesus lays down the basis for these **relationships** with two simple ideas: **love** God, and **love** your neighbour.

In the New Testament the term used to define this is 'agape'. Jesus uses the word 'love' in the sense of unconditional or unselfish love for others. This type of love is the basis of the Christian religion and the ideal way in which relationships should be lived.

The word 'love' is used in many different ways in our society. For example, a person could:

■ love their family and friends
■ love their country
■ love their partner.

In the New Testament the word 'love' is used in several different ways:

■ love in the sense of loving family and friends is philia
■ the love of country, patriotism, is storge and includes the bond between family members
■ the term for sexual love is eros.

In the English language the word 'love' is used to cover all these different forms and types of love, and it is how the word is used that gives it a meaning.

Human relationships take many forms, such as those with:

■ members of a family
■ networks of friends
■ networks of work colleagues
■ people who share a religious faith and **worship** together
■ a **community** of people who live in the same area
■ people who share a common nationality.

In all aspects of daily life people interact with each other in different ways and at different levels. All religions give guidance on how people should live their lives and provide a framework of religious beliefs and teachings about human relationships.

All the sacred texts are an important source of information on this topic. Christians use the Bible, **Jews** use the Torah and **Sikhs** use the Guru Granth Sahib.

Activities

1   Think back to the important questions on page 15.

    a   When you were writing your descriptions, did you mention anything about religion? If not, why?

    b   Do you think your religious beliefs (or lack of beliefs) are an important part of who you are?

    c   How important are shared religious beliefs for a successful marriage?

2   **a**   Copy and complete this spider diagram of the different relationships you have.

    b   Share your diagram with a partner. How does the information on your diagrams differ?

    c   As a class, use the information on your spider diagrams to talk about the different kinds of relationships you know about.

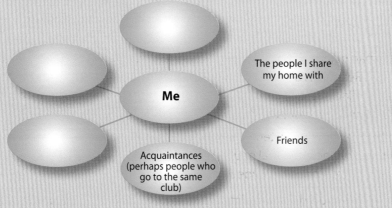

3   Try to find some song lyrics (modern and old) that deal with each of the four types of love mentioned earlier. Jot down some snatches of the lyrics. In modern songs, which type of love do you think is the most commonly used?

Sikh and Jewish views on the family

In the religion of Sikhism, family relationships are particularly important. Family life is the basis of human society and a marriage brings together two families.

In British society the small nuclear family has become the most common social unit. In Sikh families the large extended family is regarded as the traditional family unit. In Judaism the role of the family is crucial in developing religious faith; for example, families celebrate festivals together or as part of a synagogue community.

Sacred texts

Love is patient, love is kind. It does not envy, it does not boast, it is not proud. It is not rude, it is not self-seeking, it is not easily angered, it keeps no record of wrongs. Love does not delight in evil but rejoices with the truth. It always protects, always trusts, always hopes, always perseveres.

1 Corinthians 13:4–7

Do not seek revenge or bear a grudge against one of your people, but love your neighbour as yourself. I am the Lord.

Leviticus 19:18

Through love and devotion mayst Thou be known.

Guru Granth Sahib, Adi Granth

1.2 Relationships and love (2)

The next two pages will help you to:

- examine how commitment is an important aspect of human life
- analyse ways in which a religious believer might show commitment to others.

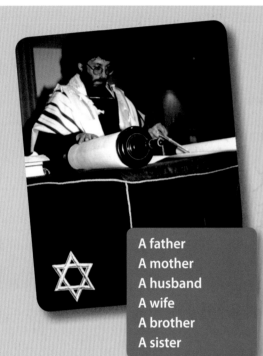

Look at these photographs. How might the person in each one show a sense of commitment? Try to give a practical example for each. Now do the same for everyone listed below.

A father
A mother
A husband
A wife
A brother
A sister

A minister
A doctor
A police officer
A school pupil
A friend
A patriot

A marathon runner
A pet shop owner
A politician
A monk or a nun
A neighbour
A high court judge

What commitments do we have to others?

Commitment is a key concept. It means a sense of dedication and obligation to someone or something. Most students will have some commitments in their day-to-day lives – even something simple like attending school or doing homework.

Religious believers can show commitment in a number of ways. They may belong to a religious community that worships and prays together. Regular **prayer**, perhaps daily, may strengthen their religious belief. Celebrating the festivals of the religion allows believers to learn more about their religion, as does reading sacred texts. Living in a way that follows the moral guidelines of their faith is one way to demonstrate commitment.

What commitments do Christians have?

Some Christians read the Bible every day. This may help to strengthen their faith and deepen their knowledge of this sacred text. The Bible is used in worship in church, and a committed Christian would want to find out more about God's relationship with humankind, so personally reading the Bible is very important. It will help a Christian to live a good life.

What commitments do Jews have?

When young Jews are ready to take on the responsibility and commitment of living as part of the Jewish faith, they make a public statement – a Bar Mitzvah for boys and a Bat Mitzvah for girls. This public statement shows they are ready to accept the Jewish commandments, which are:

- the Ten Commandments
- the 603 laws in the Torah.

What commitments do Sikhs have?

Sikhs have a strong commitment to community and **equality**. The Gurdwara, the Sikh place of worship, is where they are able to make a practical demonstration of their faith through *langar* – the sharing of free vegetarian food with everyone, regardless of religious belief.

Activities

1 With a partner, make an ideas map to show how a religious believer might show their commitment to their religion. Use the examples from the text and add some ideas of your own. You could complete this task as a general answer for religious believers or give specific examples from one religious tradition.

2 Put yourself in the shoes of a Christian, Jew or Sikh. What commitments would you have to the following? (In other words, how does a practising religious believer show their commitments to others?) Try to give three practical examples for each category listed.

- Parents
- Boyfriend/girlfriend
- Family
- Friends
- Neighbours
- Local community
- School
- Workplace
- Community in local place of worship.

Must think about!

In pairs, think about how having a religious belief might show commitment in each of the scenarios outlined below. You need to think about what a religious believer would do in these situations. What would you do? Are there any differences? If so, why?

- Walking past a *Big Issue* street collector who asks you to buy a copy of the magazine.
- Being asked to take some food to the school harvest festival celebration assembly.
- Your best friend in school telling you they have forgotten their packed lunch.
- Your mum or dad asking you to wash the dishes and do some housework.
- Your boyfriend/girlfriend forgetting to do some homework for GCSE RS and asking to borrow your book to copy up the work.

1.3 Relationships and love (3)

The next two pages will help you to:

- explore the importance of religious guidelines for all human behaviour
- express the importance of a religious upbringing for religious believers.

- **What guidelines and rules do you think we need in modern society and relationships for how we should live our lives today?**

- **Write down five new commandments.**

- **Now compare them to the Ten Commandments in Exodus 20:2–17. Are there any similarities?**

What responsibilities do we have towards each other?

Responsibility is a key concept. It means actions that we are expected to carry out. For all religious believers there has to be a sense of responsibility in how we live with other people. How we live within relationships is important.

The Ten Commandments in the Book of Exodus set out a code of behaviour for all human society. It is interesting to note that the religions of Christianity, Judaism and Sikhism would all accept the Ten Commandments as a basis for human life. These 'rules' about human behaviour are really guidelines as to how people how should live their lives; these 'guidelines' are found in commandments five to ten.

WORSHIP ONLY GOD.

DO NOT WORSHIP ANY OTHER GODS.

DO NOT MISUSE GOD'S NAME.

KEEP THE SABBATH DAY HOLY.

Activities

1   Look at the Ten Commandments.

   a   With a partner, discuss what you think each one means. Try to write down the meaning of each commandment in a modern way. (In the film *Licence to Wed*, Robin Williams plays a ten commandments game with a group of young people who do just that.)

   b   Now join with another pair and compare notes. What are the similarities? What are the differences? Try to give explanations.

What is the importance of the fifth commandment?

Look at your modern explanation of the fifth commandment. It is really about family life. Human society is based on the special nature of family life and mutual respect within the family unit. Each person has different roles and responsibilities. Within the terms of the commandments, parents have a responsibility to look after and care for their children. The care involves the physical, mental, emotional and **spiritual** well-being of any child. Christians, Jews and Sikhs would all regard it as their duty, and an important responsibility, to give their children a religious upbringing.

RESPECT YOUR PARENTS.

DO NOT COMMIT MURDER.

DO NOT COMMIT ADULTERY.

DO NOT STEAL.

DO NOT LIE.

DO NOT COVET YOUR NEIGHBOUR'S GOODS OR FAMILY.

2 Jot down three fictional families. They can come from books you have read or perhaps a TV show or film you have watched.

   a Draw a family tree to show all the members and their relationships to each other.

   b Make a note about how the family works as a 'unit'. Do the members like each other? Do any of the younger members have a problem with the older members? Do any of the older members have a problem with the younger members? What else do you know about this family? Do any family members hold any religious beliefs?

3 Pick one commandment for each member of the family that you think would help that person. Give reasons for your choice.

4 Write two paragraphs on the importance (or not) of having a religious upbringing. Your thoughts on this will contribute towards a class debate.

5 Try to answer the Grade Studio question below. When you have written it, turn to pages 36 and 37 for a full model response.

A *It is important that children are given a religious upbringing.*

B *It is not important in this day and age for children to have a religious upbringing.*

1 On your own, look at these two points of views.

   a Which one do you personally agree with?

   b In general, who do you think might agree with statement A?

   c In general, who do you think might agree with statement B?

   d Have your answers to b and c made you change your answer to a?

2 Prepare for a class debate. Divide into two groups – one to argue for statement A, and one to argue for statement B. In your groups, make a list of the main points that support your argument. Then, as a class, begin your debate. Remember to listen to the opinion of others. They may have thought of something you haven't.

3 Once the debate has finished, working on your own, jot down the key points raised by both sides. Has the debate helped you to see another point of view? Explain your answer.

Sacred texts

Train a child in the way he should go, and when he is old he will not turn from it.

Proverbs 22:6

My son, if you accept my words and store up my commands within you, turning your ear to wisdom and applying your heart to understanding, and if you call out for insight and cry aloud for understanding, and if you look for it as for silver and search for it as for hidden treasure, then you will understand the fear of the Lord and find the knowledge of God. For the Lord gives wisdom, and from his mouth come knowledge and understanding.

Proverbs 2:1–6

Hear, O Israel: The Lord our God, the Lord is one. Love the Lord your God with all your heart and with all your soul and with all your strength. These commandments that I give you today are to be upon your hearts. Impress them on your children. Talk about them when you sit at home and when you walk along the road, when you lie down and when you get up. Tie them as symbols on your hands and bind them on your foreheads. Write them on the doorframes of your houses and on your gates.

Deuteronomy 6:4–9

The word of God is true, and true are those who speak of God. Those ears are true, and true are those who listen to the Lord's praises.

Guru Granth Sahib, Guru Arjan

GradeStudio

Question

'Religious belief should be a matter of choice; parents should not teach their children about religion.'
Give two reasons why a religious believer might agree or disagree with this statement. *(4 marks)*

This question tests your ability to present a point of view and evaluate it (AO2). Examiners will use levels to measure the quality of your response. Not only will a good answer state a point of view, but it will also justify that view in detail, drawing on religious beliefs and teachings to present evidence for the view. A good answer will also recognise that there may be more than one view on the issue.

1.4 Adult relationships

The next two pages will help you to:

■ explore the religious belief that sex is a gift from God
■ analyse the religious viewpoints on sexual activity.

■ **Is there a difference in meaning between the terms 'having sex' and 'making love'?**

■ **If so, what do you think it is?**

What is the role and purpose of sex?

Within adult relationships all religions regard sexual relationships as an important part of being human. Sex is a natural part of life and allows two people to become intimate. Sex is part of God's **creation**. It is essential for reproduction and the continuation of the human race. For religious believers, sex is a special part of being human and should only be shared between two people who have a commitment to each other. A sexual relationship brings two people closer together in a special way. It is a physical expression of love. As sex is part of God's creation it is essentially a good thing only in the right situation.

Activities

1 As a class, discuss these two questions.
   a Does the mass media portray sex as something special? (Think about how magazines, television programmes, films and the Internet portray sex.)
   b How might a religious believer argue that sex should be portrayed in the mass media?

Whose decision is it concerning the use of contraception?

Contraception is a way of preventing an unwanted pregnancy. For the religious believer, contraception must never be used to encourage casual sex or promiscuity. Importantly, contraception allows a couple to control and limit the size of their family. The teachings on the use of contraception vary from one religion to another.

Christianity: Roman Catholics oppose all artificial methods of contraception, but the rhythm method, which is a natural form, is acceptable. Protestants accept all methods of contraception.

Judaism: Contraception is generally accepted. Some Jews prefer the rhythm method as a natural form of family planning. Others prefer oral contraceptives, as the man's sperm is not destroyed. Any barrier method, such as male and female condoms, is generally not accepted because it may diminish the sexual pleasure of a couple.

Sikhism: Sikhs do not oppose any forms of birth control.

Why do people choose contraception?

If you have just attempted activity 2, you will know that there are no simple answers. Modern methods of contraception have become available since the sacred texts were written. The reasons for choosing contraception are often complicated and may include:

- a couple not yet wanting to start a family
- the physical and mental health of the mother
- not wanting to increase the size of the family
- not being able to support any more children financially
- not wanting to add to human overpopulation.

What are promiscuity, adultery and cohabitation?

Promiscuity is when people have casual sexual relationships – sometimes before marriage and sometimes during. Adultery is where a married man or woman has a sexual relationship with someone other than their partner.

Christians, Jews and Sikhs all believe these lifestyle choices are wrong. In the Torah and the Bible the teaching is clear: commandment seven forbids adultery. Sikhs believe there is a spiritual union between a woman and a man within marriage, and both promiscuity and adultery would undermine this belief.

Cohabiting means living together like a married couple but without going through a marriage ceremony. The term also implies the couple are having a sexual relationship. Cohabitation raises the issue of **chastity**. Chastity means not having sex before marriage. A person may choose to be 'chaste' and remain sexually pure for marriage – as is taught in Christianity, Judaism and Sikhism.

- Many Christians choose to live like this. In fact, monks and nuns take **vows** of chastity and remain **celibate** for the rest of their lives. They do this so they can dedicate their lives to God in a life of service and prayer. Roman Catholic priests are also celibate.
- Judaism teaches that sex outside marriage is forbidden; marriage is regarded as a duty and sex should only take place within marriage.
- Sikhism teaches chastity before marriage.

Cohabitation is not accepted by all Christian denominations – there are issues of pre-marital and extra-marital sexual relationships. Because of this religious belief, cohabitation may be seen as undermining aspects of the sacred nature of a religious ceremony. Religious believers may also be concerned that cohabitation suggests a lack of commitment within a relationship.

Activities

3 Summarise the information on these complex moral topics from the point of view of what Christians believe and from the point of view of either Jews or Sikhs.

4 Try to answer the Grade Studio question opposite, then turn to pages 36–37 for advice on what constitutes a good answer.

Activities

2 Briefly discuss these questions with a partner.

a Is contraception an intimate and private matter between a woman and a man?

b Should the use of contraception be left to individual conscience?

c Is it possible to read and interpret sacred texts for guidance on this topic anyway?

d Why should a religion have a teaching on this issue? What is it to do with religious leaders?

GradeStudio

Question

'Pre-marital sex is always wrong for Christians.' Do you agree? Give reasons or evidence for your answer, showing that you have thought of more than one point of view. You must include reference to religious beliefs in your answer. *(8 marks)*

This question tests your ability to present more than one point of view and to evaluate them (AO2). Examiners will use AO2 levels to measure the quality of your response. Not only will a good answer state a point of view, but it will also justify that view in some detail. The answer must include two different points of view. The answer must also include reference to religious beliefs.

1.5 Cohabitation

The next two pages will help you to:

- evaluate the value of marriage in contemporary society
- explore different viewpoints on the themes of marriage and cohabitation.

- **Who are the people in this painting?**
- **Were they married?**

Is marriage out of date?

Contemporary society is changing and, rather than marry, many people choose to cohabit. Couples who cohabit might argue that their commitment to each other is just as strong as if they were to marry.

Some couples who cohabit may never marry, but others may eventually get married, especially if they want a family. They may decide on a religious or **secular** wedding ceremony.

Those who choose never to marry may do so to avoid the expense of a wedding or the legal problems of getting divorced. Some couples are the same sex – although these days they can have a civil partnership, which makes their relationship legally binding.

Some Christians feel it is acceptable to cohabit as part of a committed relationship, while others feel that chastity before marriage and marriage itself are essential. But, although cohabitation is more socially acceptable these days, religious believers such as Jews and Sikhs do not believe it is right to cohabit before marriage. And many believe that both cohabitation and divorce mean that marriage is no longer seen as special and for life.

Activities

1 Look at the lists below. One gives evidence and reasons to support marriage in church; the other supports cohabitation. Write down the questions these arguments could be used to answer.

Marriage in church

- It is a sacrament.
- It is a tradition.
- It is a sign of commitment.
- It is regarded as a basis for having children.
- It is regarded as a basis for family life.
- It is still popular today.

Cohabitation

- It is increasingly popular.
- Some people cohabit before marriage, giving them an opportunity to get to know each other well before going ahead with marriage.
- There is no social stigma today.
- There is a decline in religious belief.
- There is a same-sex option.
- Divorce is on the increase.

2 Find a partner, and wait to be 'named' by your teacher as either pair A or pair B.

- Pair A should jot down all the things they can think of to support the idea that marriage is *not* out of date.
- Pair B should jot down the reasons to support the idea that marriage *is* out of date.

3 Work with a different letter pair to share your lists. Help each other to complete a bullet point list of arguments 'for' and 'against'.

4 Imagine you are working as an editor for an advice column in a teen magazine. Your job is to write replies to readers' letters. A parent has written in asking for advice on how to deal with a rebellious teenager. What advice would you give to this parent? You only have space for 150 words in the column. Think about what you consider being a good parent is all about and try to work this into your reply.

Must think about!

In the examination you will be presented with a statement such as: 'Marriage is out of date; everyone should just live together today.' You will then be asked to give two reasons why a religious believer might agree or disagree with the statement.

How important is the family?

Some people would argue strongly that the family is the basic building block of society and the place where people learn about relationships. There is no real alternative to the family. No one has come up with a practical alternative to this way of living.

Within the family itself children and adults have different roles and responsibilities, and these are learned and taught within the family. Parents, for example, are role models for their children, both as adults and as women and men.

Families are not just social units; they are economic units too. Parents support their children financially until the children become young adults and are able to support themselves. An extended family provides a network of people who offer support to each other, perhaps both financially and socially.

Must think about!

Think about what courtship means. Courtship is important in the development of a relationship because it lets each partner find out about the other.

- In the Christian tradition, courtship and engagement are a public statement that the couple intend to marry after a period of time.
- In the Jewish tradition, courtship is considered a very private thing while the couple gets to know each other and only becomes public when the couple are positive the relationship has a future.
- In the Sikh tradition, the concept of courtship is different where assisted marriages take place. The couple getting married do not meet alone. In reality, though, Sikh teenagers enjoy a mixed social life as a result of living in a society where dating is a natural part of life.

1.6 Marriage

The next two pages will help you to:

- explain the most important features of a religious wedding ceremony from two religious traditions
- explore why religious believers choose to marry in a place of worship.

- **Why do you think people choose a religious wedding ceremony?**

Is it necessary to marry in a place of worship?

For Christians, marriage in church is an expression of the love the couple have for each other – a mix of agape, eros and philia. In a secular wedding ceremony only solemn promises are made. Both forms of marriage are about a public demonstration of commitment – a sense of dedication and obligation to someone or something.

When people marry, and sometimes even if they don't, they tend to make promises to each other. In religious terms, these are known as solemn vows, which are made in the presence of God – and therefore usually in a place of worship.

What happens at a Jewish wedding ceremony?

- Before the wedding the bride will visit the **mikveh**. This is an immersion pool that is used for purity and ritual cleanliness.
- On the day of the wedding the couple will **fast** to ask for God's forgiveness.
- The wedding ceremony can take place in the synagogue or outside, but is always under a **huppah** (a canopy with four poles). This is a symbol of how the couple will build a home together.

Activities

1 In pairs, look at the two wedding services below.

a One is secular (no religion) and one is Christian. Which do you think is which?

b Do these services have any similarities? And do they have any differences? Make a list of each.

You are invited to a marriage service at St John's Church Saturday, 1 June, 11 a.m.

Arrival of the bride – 'The wedding march'
Entrance hymn – 'Love divine'
Welcome – Reverend John Wayne
Address on the sacred nature of marriage

Bible Reading 1 – Old Testament
Hymn – 'Amazing grace'
Bible reading 2 – New Testament

Exchange of vows and rings
Signing of the register

Final hymn – 'Morning has broken'
Photographs

You are invited to a marriage service at Brynmawr Hotel, 11 a.m.

Champagne on arrival

Arrival of the bride – theme music to Titanic

Welcome – Registrar Julie Morgan

Address on the serious nature of marriage
Reading poem 1 – 'I love you'
Music tape – 'Love is all around'
Reading poem 2 – words written by groom

Exchange of solemn promises

Exchange of rings

Signing of the register

Reception and photographs

- The ceremony begins with two **blessings** over a cup of **wine**. The wine is a symbol of joy and happiness.
- The couple will then **drink** out of the **same wineglass** to show unity.
- The groom places a **ring** on the bride's finger to show how he will always care for her.
- Then there are readings from the *ketubah* (a marriage contract that states how the man will feed, clothe, protect, love and care for his wife).
- During the ceremony the rabbi gives a **sermon** and recites seven blessings, which thank God for creating the world and bringing joy and happiness to the couple.
- Towards the end of the ceremony the man **smashes** a **wineglass** with his heel to show how there will be good and bad times in the marriage.
- The ceremony ends with the congregation shouting '**Mazel tov**' ('Good luck').
- After the ceremony the couple spend time alone where they will break their fast. This is known as *yichud*.

What happens at a Sikh wedding ceremony?

- Sikh weddings usually take place in the morning.
- Many Sikh weddings are assisted marriages.
- The ceremony can take place in the Gurdwara or large hall but is always in the presence of the **Guru Granth Sahib**.
- The ceremony begins with musicians singing a **hymn**.
- The bride enters the room and stands on the left-hand side in front of the Guru Granth Sahib. **Men and women sit separately**.
- The couple are symbolically tied together with the **groom's scarf**.
- Four verses of the *lavan* are read out and sung as the couple walk around the Guru Granth Sahib. The **groom leads the bride** in this part of the ceremony.
- After this there is a reading from the **Guru Granth Sahib**.
- Finally everyone shares in *karah prashad*.

Christian vows

For all Christians, marriage is a serious and life-long commitment shared by two people. The marriage ceremony is a rite of passage; it marks a change in the couple's status and an important stage in their lives. For some Christians, the marriage ceremony is a sacrament where they believe God blesses the marriage by the sending of grace to the married couple. This is one of the reasons why Christians would want the marriage ceremony to take place in a church. In the marriage service there is always an exchange of vows between the couple witnessed by the Christian minister and the congregation. The minister states the vows first and then the groom and bride repeat the vows individually. The vows are exchanged between the couple and witnessed by God. These traditional vows are a solemn and public demonstration of the commitment shared by the couple.

The format and general meaning of the vows looks like this:

'… to have and to hold…   *marriage is the union of a couple*
from this day forward…   *married from this day onwards*
for better for worse…   *married for the good and bad times in life*
for richer for poorer…   *married regardless of financial status or wealth*
in sickness and in health…   *married regardless of mental or physical health*
to love and to cherish…   *love is an essential part of this special relationship*
till death do us part…'   *marriage is for life*

1.7 Separation and divorce

The next two pages will help you to:

- explore the reasons for separation and divorce in society today
- examine the religious viewpoints on separation and divorce.

- How many marriages end in separation or divorce? Can you guess?

- Now research the real figure and whether the divorce rate is going up or down.

Why do some marriages succeed and others fail?

Conflict is a key concept. It refers to the stresses and strains that take place within all human relationships. The reasons some marriages succeed and others fail are often very complex. Christians understand that there is conflict in any human relationship. Human beings are not perfect, and conflict is part of the human make-up.

Reconciliation is another key concept. It means that people are able to say sorry and make up after an argument.

However, when reconciliation is not possible between married people, there is a possibility of a separation or even divorce (the legal ending of a marriage). This is particularly painful when children are involved and decisions need to be made about which parent a child goes to live with.

Activities

1. Copy this list. Then mark on it the reasons you think help the marriage to succeed (S) and those that contribute to its failure (F).

Being 'in love'
Liking your partner
Having no children
Having an age gap between partners
Work/life balance
Crime
Unemployment
Shared hobbies
Adultery

Drug abuse
Having children
Religious faith
Money problems
Marrying young
Marrying in a place of worship
Different interests
Friends
In-laws

2. **a** Look at your S boxes. Choose the main reason you think marriages succeed.

   b Look at your F boxes. Choose the main reason you think marriages fail.

3. As a class, discuss your answers to 1 and 2, to see if you can agree on the main reasons why marriages fail or succeed.

Television research

Watch an episode of a soap opera and write down examples of the different types of conflict. You need to write a note explaining the nature of the conflict.

What are the complex issues in separation and divorce?

Christian viewpoints

There is no single Christian viewpoint on these issues and it is important to understand this. In making decisions about lifestyle, Christians may use a variety of sources for guidance. They will want to consider first the example or teaching of Jesus contained in the Gospels.

- Did Jesus say anything about marriage or divorce or sex?
- What about the teachings of Saint Paul in his letters in the New Testament?
- Does the rest of the Bible have any teachings about marriage or divorce or sex?

In looking at the teachings of Jesus and Saint Paul some Christians will argue that teachings may need to change because of changes in modern society. This is part of the debate between the liberal and traditional viewpoints. Much of this debate is about how Christians interpret religious beliefs and teachings and apply them to daily life today. Some Christians will argue that contemporary or modern society is very different from the society that Jesus lived in. The acceptance of divorce by some Christian churches changes the view that marriage is for life.

The Roman Catholic viewpoint

- It is acceptable to some Christians, such as Roman Catholics, if a couple separate and live apart.
- It is not possible to remarry without a divorce, so a couple who simply separate will not be able to remarry.
- The Roman Catholic Church does not accept divorce.

The Jewish and Sikh viewpoint

- In both Judaism and Sikhism separation and divorce are allowed.
- Marriage is a voluntary agreement between a man and a woman, so if the marriage fails a separation or divorce allows a couple to part.
- It is not usual for Sikhs to remarry if they divorce.

Activities

4   Write down the title: 'Divorce'. Under the heading write a personal statement (three or four lines) outlining what you think about this topic. Start with 'I think divorce…'.

5   Draw a table with columns headed 'For' and 'Against', and list why people should (or shouldn't) be allowed to divorce. Use some of the religious viewpoints and add some views of your own.

6   Look again at your table. How could we reduce the divorce rate in the UK? Make at least five practical suggestions.

7   Try to answer the Grade Studio question below. You will find guidance on how to build a model answer on pages 36–37.

GradeStudio

Question

Explain how having a religious faith might influence a married couple who want a divorce. *(4 marks)*

This question is asking you to consider religious viewpoints about marriage and divorce (AO1). Examiners use levels to measure student responses. Not only will a good answer describe a view, but it will also explain in some detail what it means, and will say how it links to other religious beliefs and affects the life of a religious believer.

Sacred texts

Anyone who divorces his wife and marries another woman commits adultery, and the man who marries a divorced woman commits adultery.
Luke 16:18

Suppose a woman was divorced by her first husband because he found something disgraceful about her. He wrote out divorce papers, gave them to her, and sent her away.
Deuteronomy 24:1

What is the value of a divorced woman's make-up and ornaments, when her husband has deserted her! She misses her children, her spouse, and the comforts of her husband's household. She lives in an emotional imbalance in a disturbed state.
Guru Granth Sahib 363

1.8 Remarriage

The next two pages will help you to:

■ examine the complex issues surrounding remarriage
■ explore the issues for religious believers about remarriage in a place of worship.

■ **If people have already had one unsuccessful marriage, why would they want to marry again?**

Should people be allowed to remarry?

When people marry for the first time, they may genuinely believe their marriage will last forever. If their marriage does not last forever, those people may not want to be alone and may therefore seek a new relationship. On some occasions, this relationship may be so serious that remarriage is considered.

Remarriage gives people the chance to find happiness in a new relationship. Because most humans beings like living in social groups, many of them want to share their life with someone and feel happy in the relationship.

Should remarriage be in a religious place of worship?

For some Christians remarriage becomes a controversial issue – especially if those involved want their new marriage to take place in a church or other place of worship.

■ Roman Catholics may not remarry in a Roman Catholic church because divorce is not recognised. There is an issue that the vow '…until death do us part' has been broken. Also, the priest says: 'What God has joined together let no man put asunder.' These suggest marriage should always be for life.
■ Some Church of England ministers will not remarry divorcees in church. They will give the couple a blessing after a registry office ceremony. The reasons for this are the same as for Roman Catholics.
■ Some Church of England ministers will remarry divorcees, particularly if they believe that one of the partners is an 'innocent party' (in other words, they have less blame for the breakdown of the original marriage).

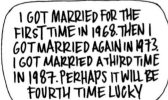

I GOT MARRIED FOR THE FIRST TIME IN 1968. THEN I GOT MARRIED AGAIN IN 1973. I GOT MARRIED A THIRD TIME IN 1987. PERHAPS IT WILL BE FOURTH TIME LUCKY

Here are the Jewish and Sikh views on remarriage:

Judaism
■ Divorce is very serious and should be the last resort.
■ Jews accept remarriage.
■ A woman is allowed to remarry after ninety days from the date of divorce.

Sikhism
■ Divorce is very serious and should be the last resort.
■ Many Sikhs accept remarriage.
■ Remarriage in a *gurdwara* is permitted.

1 Read this case study about Joanna, then complete the tasks.

Case study

Joanna was married in church at the age of 20. When she was 31 her husband Jack had an affair and left her and their two young children. Three years later she met and fell in love with Richard. He had a son from a previous marriage and had been divorced for five years.

Joanna had been a Christian since she was 13 and regularly went to her Anglican church. She did not believe in extra-marital sex and wanted to marry her new boyfriend. Richard, whom she had known for a year, was not a Christian. He decided to go to church with Joanna and her children every Sunday. The vicar of her local church was new and Joanna did not know him very well. When Joanna and Richard asked the vicar to marry them he refused. Joanna was very upset.

a Imagine you are the minister. Explain why you would not marry this couple.

b If you were Joanna and Richard what would you do? Think about the different options and make a list.

What is the secular and religious viewpoint?

It is important to understand that marriage in the UK comes in two parts.

- In a church service it is a religious ceremony, a **rite of passage** and part of the Christian tradition.
- Marriage is also an event marked by the state, so a registrar must complete a wedding certificate to show that the couple are legally married.

Therefore, a wedding certificate is not just a religious statement of marriage, it is a legal document too.

As far as the state is concerned, any divorcee may remarry in a registry office or designated place as long as the divorcee has legally divorced a previous partner. There is no limit to the number of times a person may divorce and remarry either in a registry office or in a designated place.

The issue for religious believers is that remarriage in a place of worship may harm the sacred nature of the marriage ceremony and undermine the sanctity of marriage. There is also concern that divorce undermines family life, particularly where children are involved.

Must think about!

Think about this argument: If you accept remarriage in church for divorced people, should there be a limit on the number of remarriages? Should a person who has been divorced twice or three times be allowed to continue to marry in a church?

1.9 Same-sex relationships

The next two pages will help you to:

- evaluate whether same-sex marriages should be allowed in a place of worship
- debate traditional and liberal views on same-sex marriage.

- **What do you think this picture represents?**
- **Share your ideas with a partner.**

Should same-sex marriages be allowed in a place of worship?

Activities

1 Write a letter to a national newspaper setting out your views on the issue of same-sex marriage. You must argue why same-sex relationships should or should not be allowed in a place of worship. You must use reasoned argument and evidence to support your views.

Same-sex relationships are a controversial issue for the different Christian churches today. Christians from different denominations have differing views about the subject.

Same-sex relationships and same-sex civil partnerships are complicated issues. Although people in same-sex relationships today may have a civil ceremony, it is not possible to have either a church blessing or church marriage. The traditional teaching of the Christian Church is that marriage was ordained by God for one woman and one man to be joined together.

However, as same-sex relationships are now recognised by the state, there is pressure on the various Christian churches to debate this issue. Part of the debate is to focus on how the Christian churches deal with issues in a changing society. The debate has two distinct parts.

- What is the Christian attitude to same-sex relationships?
- Should same-sex marriages be allowed in a place of worship?

How does the traditional view exclude same-sex marriage?

In the Christian tradition, marriage is regarded as the joining together of a man and a woman in church. It is a gift from God and there is the belief that sex should only take place within marriage.

Many people believe that marriage is the basis for having children, and the vows exchanged in church are a practical guideline as to how marriage should work. It is important for Christians that the marriage is blessed in the eyes of God.

Therefore, the traditional view is that same-sex relationships are wrong.

What is the liberal view?

Some Christians believe that Christian teachings need to adapt and, if necessary, change for the different society in which Christianity now finds itself.

Some think that, as Christianity is based on compassion and love (agape) for others, all people who want to marry in church should have the opportunity to do so. The compromise for same-sex relationships would be for the couple to receive a blessing in church, as is sometimes offered to people who are divorced.

What does society in general think?

In a secular society many people appear to have no religious views about the wedding ceremony or marriage itself. The divorce rate remains high in Britain and cohabitation is now common. Children may be born outside marriage and, on occasions, same-sex couples raise their own families (through artificial insemination or adoption). It would seem that views on same-sex relationships appear to be changing.

What do Jews and Sikhs think?

Some Conservative Jews do not support the idea of same-sex marriage. But other more liberal Jews prefer to leave the decision to individual rabbis.

Sikhs have no written view on same-sex relationships. That said, Sikhs generally believe in having large families, supported by a mother and father.

Activities

2 Look at the following quotes. Which ones do you agree with? You must explain why you agree or disagree with the statements.

I think that, if you are committed, then it is OK to live with someone – whether they are the same sex or not.

I believe that sex before marriage is always wrong.

I think sex is just for pleasure. You don't need commitment to have sex.

I believe that same-sex relationships are always wrong.

I think cheating on your partner is OK if you can get away with it.

If you don't go to church regularly, why do you want to get married in church – in same-sex relationships or straight relationships?

What's all the fuss about? If two people of any sex want to live together rather than get married, then why not?

1 Relationships

Remember and Reflect

The questions in this section are based on the work you have done throughout this topic. Try to complete as many as you can.

The questions in set 1 are designed to test your factual recall and AO1 level skills (knowledge and understanding). The page numbers alongside the questions will help you to find information that might be useful for your answers. Use them to check against what you have written.

The questions in set 2 are more challenging, using AO2 level skills (use of evidence and reasoned argument to evaluate personal responses and differing viewpoints). Your answers may come from more than one part of the topic.

Set 1 – knowledge and understanding

1	Explain what each of the following key words means in one sentence: **a** love **b** relationships **c** commitment **d** conflict **e** reconciliation.	pages 14–15
2	Give two different types of love.	pages 16–17
3	Give two examples of commitment in human relationships.	pages 18–19
4	Do you think the Ten Commandments about human behaviour are relevant in society today? If yes, why? If not, why not? Give reasons.	pages 20–21
5	Give two purposes of sex.	pages 22–23
6	Give three reasons why some people live celibate lives.	pages 22–23

Set 2 – use of evidence and personal response

1 Answer the following questions, giving as much detail in your answers as possible.

   a Are you a religious believer? Give at least three reasons to support your answer.

   b Do you think chastity has a place in modern society? Explain your answer fully.

   c Do you think parents should influence the religious beliefs of their children? Why or why not?

   d Do you think marriage ceremonies should only take place in places of worship? Explain why you think this.

2 Copy and complete the table below, showing how a Christian, a Jew and a Sikh might respond to the issues given in the table. (Remember, not all religious believers agree on everything so try to reflect this in your answers, particularly within the Christian religion.) You could try drawing a Venn diagram, joining together all three religious traditions to identify any common ground. Make sure you include reference to religious knowledge and give as many reasons for each view as possible in the columns provided.

Issue	What would a Christian say and why?	What would a Jew say and why?	What would a Sikh say and why?
The value of courtship before marriage			
Sex before marriage (pre-marital sex)			
Sex outside marriage (extra-marital sex)			
Same-sex relationships			

GradeStudio

On these pages you will find the types of questions you might encounter in your exam, along with sample answers, mark schemes and examiner comments. A good understanding of this information may help you to improve the content and structure of your own answers. It will also help you to understand what the examiner is looking for and how to improve your marks in the exam.

Question

Explain how having a religious faith might influence a married couple who want a divorce.

(4 mark question, AO1)

This question asks you to consider religious viewpoints about marriage and divorce (AO1). Examiners use levels to measure student responses. Not only will a good answer describe a view, but it will also explain in some detail what it means and will say how it links to other religious beliefs and affects the life of a religious believer. You could build an answer like this:

Level 1	**Level 2**
A simple link between beliefs and practices.	An explicit link between beliefs and practices. Limited use of specialist language.
Level 3	**Level 4**
Analysis showing some awareness and insight into religious facts, ideas, practices and explanations. Uses and interprets a range of religious language and terms.	Coherent analysis showing awareness and insight into religious facts, ideas, practices and explanations. Uses religious language and terms extensively and interprets them accurately.

Student's answer

A lot of religions don't believe in divorce. They think that once you are married you should stay married. This is because the Bible tells them this. (Level 1)

Examiner's comments

This student has reached Level 1 by making a very basic statement about religion and marriage, demonstrating they understand the question. It could have been improved by explaining that Christians, Jews and Sikhs all believe that marriage is important and special, and that divorce is a last resort. There has to be a simple link between religious belief and practice for a Level 1 mark.

To achieve Level 2, the student could link between beliefs and practices with some use of specialist vocabulary. For example, if the student says that some Christians think marriage is a sacrament, this is use of specialist vocabulary. If the student says a Jewish couple might ask the advice of the rabbi, this too is specialist vocabulary.

To reach Level 3, the student needs to show an awareness of and insight into religious practices and explanations; they would need to show both the significance of marriage for the religious tradition and give examples of how this belief would influence a decision about marriage. They might refer to the significance of the Christian wedding vows, and to a couple asking for prayers and help from a local faith community to support them in a marriage.

Finally, to reach the top level, the student needs to show a real awareness of and insight into religious ideas, practice and explanations. The answer needs to be comprehensive, giving evidence of religious language and terms being used extensively throughout. The student needs to show clear a understanding of the question and provide a detailed answer.

Student's improved answer

A lot of religions don't believe in divorce. Christians, Jews and Sikhs all believe that marriage is important and special, and that divorce should be a last resort. Roman Catholics don't think you should get divorced at all. (Level 1)

When people get married in a religious service, they are making a commitment that they will always stay together. But these days that isn't always possible. Religious believers may decide to stay together rather than get divorced, even though they are not happy. Others might separate, but not get divorced or remarried. (Level 2)

Some Christians think that marriage is a sacrament. They get married in a church in the eyes of God, and make special vows, which say they will be faithful to each other until they are parted by death. So, even when things get tough in their marriage, they will not get a divorce. (Level 3)

Some Jews will accept divorce. A Jewish couple might be able to ask their rabbi what they think about getting divorced. Deuteronomy 24:1 says:
'When a man hath taken a wife, and married her, and it come to pass that she find no favour in his eyes, because he hath found some uncleanness in her: then let him write her a bill of divorcement, and give it in her hand, and send her out of his house.' (Level 4)

Question

'Pre-marital sex is always wrong for Christians.' Do you agree? Give reasons or evidence for your answer, showing that you have thought of more than one point of view. You must include reference to religious beliefs in your answer. **(8 mark question, AO2)**

This question tests your ability to present more than one point of view and to evaluate them (AO2). Examiners will use AO2 levels to measure the quality of your response. Not only will a good answer state a point of view, but it will also justify that view in some detail. The answer must include two different points of view. The answer must also include reference to religious beliefs. See page 11 for level descriptors for 8 mark AO2 questions.

Student's answer

I do not agree with this statement, because it is a natural part of life, there is no law against it and if the two people feel it is right then no one else should have a problem. (Level 1)

Examiner's comments

This student gives a simple point of view, linked to the example of the legal situation and how two people might feel about sex before marriage. It is a very weak Level 1.

To achieve a higher level the student needs to develop the answer with some reference to religious teaching and make a connection between the statement and in this case the direct reference to the Christian religion.

To reach Level 3 the student needs to write in more detail with specialist language included in the answer. At this level there should be recognition of a different point of view.

To achieve a Level 4 the student needs to use specialist language, include reasons for and against the statement, and include reference to religious teachings and moral aspects at issue for the individual or society.

Student's improved answer

I think pre-marital sex is always wrong in a Christian's eyes because some Christians have claimed that God has said that it is wrong in the Bible. (Level 1)

At the time of Jesus all Jews believed that sex before marriage was wrong. In the vows fidelity is one of the ideas; one partner for life. We should follow our religion properly and do good things and this means to live in chastity before marriage. (Level 2)

Sex is a gift from God and should only be expressed in marriage where eros may take place. Other people may be Christians and want sex and children before marriage. They think that as long as you are in a committed relationship this is OK. (Level 3)

No Christians believe that promiscuity is right. I think that in God's eyes this is wrong. If you are a Christian then you should follow your religion properly and listen to God. (Level 4)

2 Is it fair?

The Big Picture

- In this topic you will be addressing issues of justice and equality.
- This topic covers three principal religions: Christianity, Islam and Buddhism.
- You will need to focus on at least two principal religions.

You will look at:

- human dignity, what it means, and whether it is something everyone has a right to
- why some people are treated differently, the reasons behind prejudice and how the media influences attitudes
- what equality really means and whether it is ever possible
- wealth, what people want and what people need
- what is fair in the world and what is unfair.

You will also think about the ways in which religious believers act on issues such as poverty, injustice, prejudice and inequality.

What?

You will:

- examine key concepts relevant to the topic
- discuss examples of prejudice and discrimination, and consider religious responses to injustice
- study religious attitudes towards wealth and resources.

Why?

Because:

- learning key concepts will help you to communicate your answers and express your own views
- studying examples of prejudice and discrimination will help you to develop your own sense of justice
- understanding religious beliefs can help you to understand why believers think and act in the ways they do.

How?

By:

- applying the key concepts to everyday situations
- studying modern-day examples of prejudice and discrimination, and applying religious teachings to these situations
- examining religious responses to injustice, including the misuse of wealth.

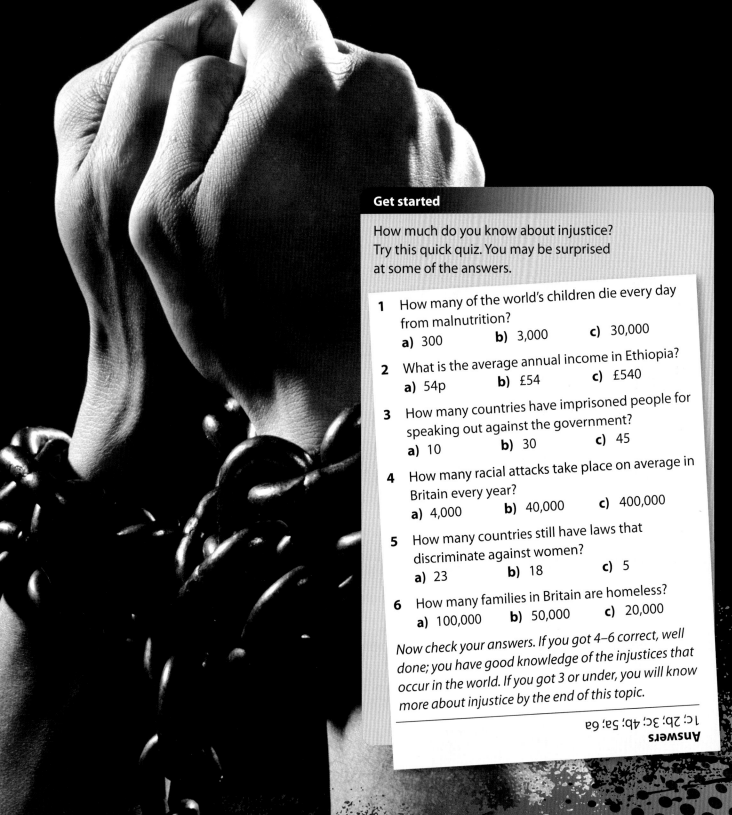

Get started

How much do you know about injustice? Try this quick quiz. You may be surprised at some of the answers.

1   How many of the world's children die every day from malnutrition?
    a) 300   **b)** 3,000   **c)** 30,000

2   What is the average annual income in Ethiopia?
    a) 54p   **b)** £54   **c)** £540

3   How many countries have imprisoned people for speaking out against the government?
    a) 10   **b)** 30   **c)** 45

4   How many racial attacks take place on average in Britain every year?
    a) 4,000   **b)** 40,000   **c)** 400,000

5   How many countries still have laws that discriminate against women?
    a) 23   **b)** 18   **c)** 5

6   How many families in Britain are homeless?
    a) 100,000   **b)** 50,000   **c)** 20,000

Now check your answers. If you got 4–6 correct, well done; you have good knowledge of the injustices that occur in the world. If you got 3 or under, you will know more about injustice by the end of this topic.

Answers
1c; 2b; 3c; 4b; 5a; 6a

Develop Your Knowledge

This topic is about the issues of justice and equality. Read the information below, which will help you to think about these issues before you begin more detailed work.

Key information

- Depending on who they are and where they are, human beings can live very different kinds of lives – from very comfortable, to just managing to survive.

- Lack of human dignity, injustice, discrimination and inequality are all issues that greatly concern religious believers.

- Many people, including religious believers, work hard to make the world a fairer place to live in; they do this through giving money and giving time.

- Issues of equality, prejudice, injustice, poverty and wealth are global – they are not just confined to the country we live in.

- Religious believers use their sacred texts as the basis for action to achieve a fairer society and a fairer world.

- Many individuals and organisations help to promote social justice and equality – perhaps encouraging others to think about what they want versus what they actually need.

- The media, which is all around us these days, can represent issues of justice and equality in many different ways, often persuading us to have a particular viewpoint.

- Each religion has much to offer about how we can give people human dignity, and deal with issues such as discrimination and injustice.

Key words

authority power over others through position or moral teaching

community group of people who are joined together because they share something in common

discrimination treating groups of people differently or unfairly

duty a moral or religious obligation

equality state in which everyone has equal rights

human dignity treating all human beings with respect regardless of race, sex or social position

human rights rights to the basic things we need in life in order to exist

identity sense of who you are in terms of attitudes, character and personality

injustice where everyone is not treated with fairness

karma the Buddhist belief that a person's deeds affect their past, present and future experiences

need something that is necessary to survive; without it, we would experience difficulties or hardship

prejudice judging people to be inferior or superior without cause

respect consideration for others; understanding that everyone has value even though their circumstances may be different

stereotype the idea that, if people wear certain types of clothes, for example, or drive certain cars, they must all have similar behaviours and values

want something we wish for, but not having it wouldn't bring hardship or poverty

Key questions

- What do we want?
- Why do people treat others differently?
- Is equality possible?
- What should be people's attitudes towards wealth?
- What do we need?
- How should we treat others?
- How does the media influence attitudes?
- Why are people prejudiced?
- What is fair?
- What is unfair?

For interest

- In the 1970s, rich northern hemisphere countries, such as Britain and the USA, lent money to poorer countries.
- Huge interest rates were added to the loans.
- Poor countries are still struggling to pay back the interest, even though they have repaid the money borrowed many times over.
- This leaves poorer countries with little money for education and healthcare.

Should Britain drop the debt? (This may mean that taxes in Britain will increase to make up for the lack of interest being paid by the poorer countries.)

Would you be prepared to become poorer so that the poor can become richer?

2.1 The background

The next two pages will help you to:

- explain what is meant by 'want'
- explore how our wants may differ from other people's wants.

What do you want? Is it things? Is it world peace? Is it to be happy? Is it to be a better person? Or is it, perhaps, to be more committed to your religion?

I want to leave school now and get a job. Joel, aged 14

I want to go to university. I wish I had tried harder to get good GCSEs. Asma, aged 19

I want to help out at the homeless shelter. I think that is what God wants me to do. Joshua, a religious believer

I just want five minutes' peace and quiet! Jamani, aged 42

I want to win the lottery so I can buy a bigger house and take my children on holiday. Emma, aged 35

What do we want?

A 'want' can be described as something we wish for, but *not* having it wouldn't bring hardship or poverty.

We often say that we 'want' something. At the time, it probably seems very important, or even essential. However, the things we want or wish for may be very different to what people in other countries may want. Our 'wants' can also differ between age groups. The things religious believers want may be different from the things people without faith may want.

Activities

1   Think again about the questions on the facing page.

   a   List five things that you want.

   b   In pairs, explain to your partner why you want these things.

2   **a**   Imagine you are a poor person living in Africa and that you are not a religious believer. What things would be on your list of 'wants'?

   b   Now think about what you would have on your list if you were a religious believer.

3   Read the statements below. Which do you most agree with? Explain why.

> I want to do well at school.

> I want to have fun at school.

> I want the best trainers.

> I want to watch TV without charity adverts making me feel guilty.

> I want to do something to help others.

In this topic, we will examine more closely examples of people who 'want' things. Sometimes people want things so badly that they are willing to go to extreme lengths to get them. This may be a good thing. For example, many religious believers have wanted equal rights for everyone, regardless of race, sex, age or gender. Unfortunately, wanting things can also lead to greed and selfishness – for example, when people want more money or more power.

At the end of this topic, we will revisit the idea of 'wants'. Perhaps the things on your own 'want' list will have changed!

Activities

4   As a class, undertake a survey of all the students. Classify the wants of the students into three categories:

   ■   personal (for example, things for themselves, such as more money)

   ■   family/friends (for example, wanting a loved one to get better)

   ■   global (for example, less flooding, fewer natural disasters).

   Which category contained the most wants? Can you think of a reason why?

For debate

A   *Life would be far better if we had whatever we wanted.*

B   *Life would be far worse if we had whatever we wanted.*

1   On your own, look at these two points of view.

   a   Which one do you personally agree with?

   b   In general, who do you think might agree with statement A?

   c   In general, who do you think might agree with statement B?

   d   Have your answers to b and c made you change your answer to a?

2   Prepare for a class debate. Divide into two groups – one to argue for statement A, and one to argue for statement B. In your groups, make a list of the main points that support your argument. Then, as a class, begin your debate. Remember to listen to the opinions of others. They may have thought of something you haven't.

3   Once the debate has finished, working on your own, jot down the key points raised by both sides. Has the debate helped you to see another point of view? Explain your answer.

2.2 Human dignity

- Look at the illustration.
- Does 'dignity' mean the same thing to both people?
- How would you define 'dignity'?

The next two pages will help you to:

- express what is meant by human dignity
- identify why not all people are treated with 'dignity'.

LOOK AT THE WAY SHE IS DRESSED! DOESN'T SHE HAVE ANY DIGNITY?!

I WISH HE COULD BE ALLOWED TO DIE WITH DIGNITY

Why do people treat others differently?

At the core of every religious tradition is the belief that all humans are worthy of honour and respect. This is known as human dignity. But sometimes people are not treated with dignity. They may be treated differently because:

- their skin is a different colour
- they have a different religion
- they live in a different area or community
- they have less money than other people
- they have more money than other people.

Why should we treat others with honour and respect?

All religions teach that we deserve to be treated with honour and respect because humans have:

- emotions
- a sense of morality
- a right to basic needs (human rights)
- **souls**
- a sense of identity.

Our sense of identity defines who we are. All humans are unique and have a unique identity. It is this uniqueness that makes each of us worthy of respect.

What does religion say?

- Christianity teaches the importance of human dignity. The Bible's account of Creation demonstrates that humans are important, as they were created in God's image, and given **dominion** (kingship) over animals and the rest of God's creation. Genesis 1:26–28: 'Then God said, "Let us make man in our image"… and God said to them, "Be fruitful and multiply, and fill the earth and subdue it."'
- Islam's teachings demonstrate that humans are the most important and highest of Allah's creations. However, they do not state that they were created in Allah's image. The Qur'an (6:165) says: 'He has made you His ruling agents in the earth.'
- In **Buddhism**, only humans have the ability to attain Buddha status and therefore be worthy of respect in their current lives. The Buddhist mantra Om Mani Padme Hung contains the words: 'May all realise their true spiritual nature and thus awaken the Buddha within.'

Activities

1 Look at the bullet list above. What other points could be added?

2 In groups, read the Declaration of Human Rights on page 45.

   a Which human rights do you have?

   b What about a child living in Africa or Asia? Do they have the same rights as you?

   c Why would a religious believer say that everyone should have human rights?

One of the key beliefs in all religious traditions is that humans are worthy of honour and respect because they are entitled to human rights. The Universal Declaration of Human Rights was produced by the United Nations in 1948. Its purpose was to ensure that all humans have the things they are entitled to or need. The Declaration states:

> All human beings are born free and equal in dignity and rights. They are endowed with reason and conscience, and should act towards one another in a spirit of brotherhood.

Why don't we all have human rights?

Not all people are given human rights. This often means they are not treated with dignity, or are treated differently from others. There are many reasons for this.

- They may live in a poor country that cannot provide basic needs such as healthcare and housing.
- The government of the country may be unjust (unfair).
- They may have broken the law or threatened the safety of others. (Sometimes governments see it as necessary to take away people's human rights in order to protect others.)

Because of their belief in human dignity, many religions see it as their duty to promote justice and fair treatment of all humans, and to ensure that all people are treated with equality.

Activities

3 a Write an answer to this exam question: '*All humans deserve to be treated with respect.' Give two reasons why a religious believer would agree or disagree with this statement.*

b Now look at the example answer in Grade Studio below. How does it compare with yours?

GradeStudio

Question

'All humans deserve to be treated with respect.'
Give two reasons why a religious believer would agree or disagree with this statement. *(4 marks)*

This question tests your ability to present religious views about a statement and explain the reasons behind those views (AO2). Examiners will use levels to measure the quality of your response. A good answer will not only state a view, but will also justify that view in detail, using religious beliefs and teachings to present evidence for the view. A good answer will also recognise that there may be more than one view about the issue.

In the table below, the left-hand column shows what examiners are looking for at the different levels. The right-hand column shows how we might build an answer.

Level 1 A simple appropriate justification of a point of view.	First, show you understand the question and state an opinion. For example, 'A religious believer may agree because sacred texts refer to human dignity.'
Level 2 An expanded justification of one point of view, which includes religious teaching OR two simple points of view.	Next, justify this view using religious teachings. For example, 'In Christianity, the Genesis account of Creation says that humans were given power or dominion over animals. Therefore all humans are worthy of respect.'
Level 3 An expanded justification of one point of view, with appropriate example and/or illustration, which includes religious teaching. In addition, a second simple appropriate justification of a point of view.	Then, offer a deeper explanation of the first point and add a second opinion. For example, 'A Buddhist would also agree because their religion teaches the idea of treating all humans with respect.'
Level 4 An expanded justification of two viewpoints, incorporating the religious teaching and moral aspects at issue and their implications for the individual and the rest of society.	Finally, develop the second viewpoint to include a religious teaching to support it. For example, 'Buddhists would say all humans are worthy of respect because humans have souls. It is only humans who have the ability to achieve Buddha status. Therefore, all humans should be treated with respect.'

2.3 Equality

The next two pages will help you to:

- analyse what is meant by 'equality'
- give examples of equality and inequality in the world.

- **Read the extract. What inequalities does Sojourner Truth mention?**
- **Do you think they still exist?**

And ain't I a woman?
I could work and eat as much as a man –
when I could get to it – and bear the lash as well!
And ain't I a woman?
I have born 13 children,
and seen most all sold into slavery,
and when I cried out with my mother's grief,
none but Jesus heard me!
And ain't I a woman?
Then that little man in black there,
he says women can't have as much rights as men,
'cause Christ wasn't a woman!

By Sojourner Truth (1797–1883), a former slave and campaigner for women's rights

Activities

1   What inequalities do you think exist today?

   a   Make a list of five things.

   b   Compare your list with a partner. Are there any similarities? Can you explain the differences?

   c   As a class, agree on a list of the three most serious inequalities.

2   Use a search engine to find a copy of the Brant Equation. Make a list of the inequalities highlighted by the report.

Is equality possible?

Inequality happens the world over in many different ways. These inequalities could be something very simple – such as pocket money or bed times between brothers and sisters. Or they could be complex, such as differences in income, education and healthcare in different parts of the world.

In the news, we often hear stories about people or countries that do not have the same rights as others.

Perhaps in our own lives we feel we have not been given the same rights or treatment as others. Why is this? Is it possible for humans to be equal?

Most religions teach that humans should be treated *fairly* (with dignity) because they are part of God's creation. This implies that humans should be treated *equally*.

Equality is the state in which everyone has equal rights. When this is not achieved, the result is inequality.

Activities

3   **a**   Look at this pie chart. How does it show that poorer countries are unequal to richer countries?

   b   List any other ways in which you feel they are not equal to richer countries.

Infant deaths per 1000 births

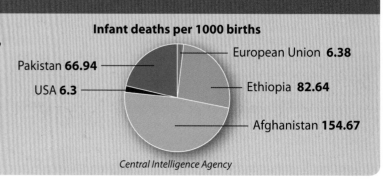

Pakistan **66.94**

USA **6.3**

European Union **6.38**

Ethiopia **82.64**

Afghanistan **154.67**

Central Intelligence Agency

What do religions teach about equality?

Christianity

Christians believe that all people are equal, as all humans come from Adam and Eve – God's creation. All humans were created in God's image, which makes them equal. Jesus' own example of helping lepers and outcasts, and befriending women, for example, shows that equality is important in Christianity. Although the Christian Church states that all humans are equal, some argue that it does not practise this teaching. For example, the Roman Catholic Church does not allow female priests, arguing that Jesus began this tradition when he chose 12 male disciples.

Islam

Muslims believe that all people are equal, though not the same – they may have different roles to play. Humans were created by Allah (God). Allah's prophet, Muhammad, showed in his actions that everyone should be treated equally. The *Ummah* (brotherhood) accepts Muslims from all nations, cultures and races. During prayer, individuals stand shoulder to shoulder to show equality before God. During *Hajj* (pilgrimage), Muslims wear *Ihram* (white garments) to show equality before God. It is becoming acceptable for Muslim women to go to work. Khaijah, Prophet Muhammad's first wife, was a successful businesswoman. Even so, some argue that, in Islam, men and women are not equal. Women sit separately from men at the mosque, and are not required to wear *Ihram* during *Hajj* (although most do).

Buddhism

Buddhists believe that all humans have a 'Buddha nature' – the potential to achieve enlightenment. Buddhism stresses the need to practise 'equanimity', which means seeing yourself as equal to others. Buddhism does not practise the 'caste system', which is sometimes used as a way of grouping people according to their social status.

For debate

In groups, discuss these questions.

- Can girls play football with boys?
- If a couple split up, who would gain custody of the children?
- Are people who have a private education more likely to succeed?

Make sure some of you argue from the opposite viewpoint.

Sacred texts

There is neither Jew nor Greek, there is neither slave nor free, there is neither male nor female; for you are all one in Christ Jesus.
Galatians 3:28

And their Lord hath accepted of them, and answered them: 'Never will I suffer to be lost the work of any of you, be he male or female: Ye are members, one of another.'
'The Holy Qur'an, translated by Yusuf Ali' *Surah 3:195*

In all things, there is neither male nor female.
Holy teaching of Vimalakirti 7 (Mahayana text)

Research note

Find out which religions allow women to become religious teachers, leaders or members of the clergy. Did any of your findings surprise you?

Activities

2 Most religious teachings state that people should be treated equally. But is this possible? List a few thoughts about this, or draw a picture that explains your viewpoint.

3 Read this teaching from the Bible. Then look at the photograph. Do you think they agree with each other? Why? Why not?

4 The editor of your school magazine has asked you to write an article entitled 'Humans can never be truly equal'.

> I permit no woman to teach or to have authority over a man; she is to keep silent.
> *1 Timothy 2:12*

   a Think about whether you agree with this statement.

   b Using the information on these two pages, plus your own ideas and any other supporting information, write your piece.

2.4 Wealth and charity

The next two pages will help you to:

- consider and explain religious attitudes towards the use of wealth
- explore why many religious believers feel it is important to make charitable donations.

- **What is your first reaction to the contents of this photograph? Be honest (at least with yourself).**

What should be people's attitudes towards wealth?

It seems that, these days, the topic of money is never far away. We hear about the global economy, the very rich and the very poor. We hear definitions of wealth such as 'the super rich' on the one hand and 'abject poverty' or 'living on the breadline' on the other. We might even struggle to understand why those with enormous wealth can't solve the problems of those in poverty.

Many religious believers see wealth as a gift rather than a right. If they have money, they feel it is their duty to use it to help others get the things they 'need'. All religious traditions teach that it is a duty to help others in need.

What attitude do religions have towards wealth?

Christianity

Christians believe that wealth is God-given, and that money will not give your life meaning. Most Christians do not gamble; some will not even do the lottery. If they lend money to others, they do not charge interest.

Christians believe that material wealth should be shared with others (such as giving to charity). They do this to show love and compassion to those in need, and because generosity should involve some sacrifice for the person who is giving. Christians try to follow the example of Jesus, who often did charitable work. Many of them 'tithe', which means they give 10 per cent of their income to the Church or to the less fortunate. They believe their generosity will be rewarded with a place in heaven.

Islam

Muslims believe that all wealth is a gift from Allah, and they should not gain money through dishonest means such as bribery or blackmail. Lending for profit is not allowed. The Qur'an says gambling, extravagance and waste are haram (forbidden). Because of this teaching, many Muslims do not take part in the lottery.

Muslims believe the more money they have, the more generous they should be. They are expected to pay *zakat* (2.5 per cent of earnings), which is one of the Five Pillars of Islam. *Sadaqah* is a voluntary charitable payment that Muslims can also make. Islam teaches that sharing and not being greedy will be rewarded on the Day of Judgement.

Activities

1   Look at these two Bible extracts. Do they both say the same thing? Explain your answer.

> Do not store up for yourselves treasures on earth… but store up for yourselves treasures in heaven.
> *Matthew 6:19–20*

> It is easier for a camel to go through the eye of a needle than for someone who is rich to enter the kingdom of God.
> *Matthew 19:24*

Activities

2 Read this hadith (ask someone to explain 'hadith' if you are not sure):

> He is not a believer who eats his fill while his neighbour remains hungry by his side.

a Write down in your own words what you understand by it.
b Now discuss with a partner. Did your answers differ? How?

Buddhism

Buddhists believe that wealth does not guarantee happiness, nor is it permanent. The Four Noble Truths advise against greed, as suffering comes from desire. The Middle Way says we should learn to find a balance between wealth and poverty.

Bhikkus (Buddhist monks) are not allowed to possess money. It is therefore seen as a good thing for lay people to support them. They often make donations of money and food to support the *sangha* (Buddhist romantic community). Buddhists believe that they will gain good karma through acts of kindness. Charitable works are a way of doing this.

Activities

3 Read this teaching of the Buddha:

> It is not fitting not to give at all … One who eats alone eats unhappily.

a Write down in your own words what you think it means.
b Now compare your definition with a partner. Do you both think the same thing?
4 Use Grade Studio to help you write a full-mark answer to this exam question: *Explain how having religious faith might encourage someone to give to charity.*

What do we need?

A 'need' can be described as something that is necessary. Without it, we would experience difficulties or hardship. Worldwide, many people do not have everything they 'need'. For many religious believers, ensuring people have the things they 'need' to survive is a basic duty. Most religions teach that giving to charity is a good thing to do. This ensures that more people have the things they 'need'.

Activities

5 Make your own list of the things we 'need' to live without hardship.
6 Look back at the information on these two pages. Design a poster (with words and pictures) that describes the teachings about wealth and its uses for two religious traditions.

GradeStudio

Question

Explain how having religious faith might encourage someone to give to charity.
(4 marks)

This question tests your ability to explain a religious point of view (AO1). Examiners use levels to measure the responses. A good answer will not only give a statement about what a religious believer thinks, but it will also explain in some detail how having religious belief links to what religious people do.

You could build an answer like this:

Level 1

First, give a reason why religious believers might give to charity. For example, 'Religious believers might give to charity because they think they should help others. This is what their religion tells them.'

Level 2

Next, make a clear link between the teachings on charity and what a believer might do. For example, 'In Islam, it is one of the Five Pillars (requirements) that all Muslims should give charitable donations. So a Muslim's faith would mean that they have to give to charity.'

Level 3

Then, describe another reason why a religious believer might give to charity. Try to bring in religious language. For example, 'Having faith would encourage believers to give to charity because sacred texts, such as the Bible, teach that giving to charity will earn a place in heaven.'

Level 4

Finally, make sure you have described in detail the teaching that inspires believers to give to charity. Try to make good use of religious terms and interpret them correctly. For example, 'The Bible says, "Store up for yourselves treasures in heaven", which suggests that giving to charity will earn a place in heaven. Therefore following sacred texts would encourage believers to give to charity.'

2.5 Social responsibility

The next two pages will help you to:

- explain why religious believers think it is important to be socially responsible
- give examples of how a religious believer can be socially responsible.

Do you recognise these logos? Jot down a few words about what they tell you.

How should we treat others?

All religious believers think it is their duty to have social responsibility. This includes showing concern for those in need – be it due to:

- poverty
- unfair treatment from others
- not being given their human rights.

Case study : I am a Christian...

Genesis 1:26 says that humans were created in God's image, which means we are all special and should be treated with respect. The Bible instructs me to care for others, so I see it as my duty to care for those in need. Jesus fed the hungry, healed the sick and treated everyone with respect. As a Christian, I believe I should follow his example.

Case study : I am a Muslim...

Allah created all humans, which means we are all important and must be cared for. The *Ummah* (brotherhood) extends to all of us who follow Islam. We are taught that it is the responsibility of the *Ummah* to care for others. The Prophet Muhammad spoke out against injustice, and we must try to follow this teaching. He encouraged others to help those who were affected by war – for example, widows whose husbands had been killed.

Case study : I am a Buddhist...

I don't believe in a god, so I don't believe God created humans. But I still need to show concern for all humans. The Buddha helped the less fortunate (beggars and slaves) as he travelled around India spreading the Dharma (teachings). The law of karma teaches cause and effect. I believe that, as a Buddhist, if I do good deeds, good things will happen to me in the future. The Eightfold Path to Enlightenment states that we should show kindness to others, and the Buddhist teaching of *metta* means loving kindness.

How do believers fight injustice?

Because religions teach the ideas of human dignity and social responsibility, many believers try to fight **injustice** in the world as a response to these teachings. They see it as their duty to help those in need.

Many charities and organisations have been set up by religious believers in an attempt to eliminate injustice. Other religious charities try to alleviate poverty. All these charities recognise that material wealth should be shared so that everyone has the things they need.

Most religious traditions teach that violence is not the way to solve issues of injustice. Therefore, religious believers try to campaign peacefully.

Activities

1 Look at the above case studies, which outline how Christians, Muslims and Buddhists think they should treat others.

   a List any similarities.

   b Now list the differences.

What are the religious charities?

Christian Aid: tries to follow the teachings of Jesus.

Salvation Army: a Christian charity that runs soup kitchens, homeless shelters and charity shops to help the poor.

Muslim Aid: follows Islamic teachings about social responsibility.

Rokpa: follows the Buddhist requirement to treat everyone with *metta* (loving kindness).

Activities

2   Look at the list of peaceful campaigns to end injustice below.

Campaigns without violence
- Praying for those in need.
- Collecting money for charities.
- Organising petitions.
- Organising protest marches.
- Being involved in a campaign such as Jubilee 2000, set up to persuade the government to drop the debt owed by developing (poorer) countries.

a   Which methods do you think would be the best to stop injustice?

b   Which methods would not be good ways to stop injustice?

Try to give reasons for your answers.

3   Make a list of any other forms of peaceful protest you can think of. Compare notes with a partner.

Sacred texts

A new commandment I give to you, that you love one another even as I have loved you.
John 13:34

Believers, stand up firmly for justice, as witnesses for Allah.
Surah 4:135

Animosity does not eradicate animosity. Only by loving kindness is animosity dissolved.
This law is ancient and eternal.
Dhammapada 1:5

Religion	Charity	Aims	Projects
Christianity	Christian Aid	• To deliver real practical benefits. • To speak out where there is injustice. • To campaign for change.	*Working in Africa* • Working with HIV/AIDS victims, providing schooling and healthcare to victims of the disease. *Working in Mozambique* • Encouraging civilians to trade weapons for farming equipment.
Islam	Muslim Aid	• To prove emergency relief and sustainable development programmes that tackle the root causes of poverty.	*Working in 70 countries in Africa, Asia and Europe* • Working with the 'Love Water, Love Life' campaign to dig wells to provide clean water for people in countries such as Kenya and Bangladesh.
Buddhism	Rokpa	• To help where help is needed.	*Working in Nepal* • Running soup kitchens for the poor. • Opening children's homes for abandoned children. • Running workshops to educate women.

Activities

4   You have been asked to compile some information about religious charities and what they do. Using the information on these pages and the table on the left, draw your own table or create a leaflet about Christian Aid plus one other charity. (Remember, you will need to be able to write about these issues in detail in your exam.)

5   Describe the work of a religious charity or organisation that has worked to alleviate poverty.

2.6 The media

The next two pages will help you to:

- give examples of the way the media influences people
- evaluate why the media may want to influence people.

- **How does the media influence issues such as prejudice and discrimination?**
- **How does it portray issues of injustice?**
- **Do we really get the full story?**

How does the media influence attitudes?

'The media' is the term we use to cover newspapers, magazines, television, radio and the Internet, all of which report on world news and affairs. We are kept up to date with issues of justice and injustice almost as soon as they occur, no matter where in the world the events take place. However, people have begun to question how accurate the media really is.

Through its use of headlines, photographs, moving images, sound and points of view, the media can influence how we understand events. Two stories, told from two points of view, can often make us believe first one side, and then the other. But why would the media want to do this? Generally, it is to make us agree with a particular point of view – and the reasons for this are complicated. It could be to influence us politically, or to prod our consciences about something, or to hide more disturbing facts from us.

When we are reading or listening to the media, we should try to answer these questions, which will help us to understand why we are being led towards a particular point of view.

Activities

1 On your own, jot down why you think a story might be told in different ways by different newspapers. Compare your answers with those of a partner. Did you list the same things?

2 Imagine you see a photograph like this on the front of a newspaper. How do you think it portrays issues of injustice?

Consider the following:

a Who is the audience?
b What are we being told?
c What information are we being given?
d Who is telling the story?
e Who is the storyteller working for or representing?
f How might this affect how the story is being told?

What is propaganda?

It is often claimed that the media does not always give an accurate view. The same story can be reported in many different ways, depending on who is writing it and why. Newspapers and news programmes have sometimes been described as using propaganda (selecting information or missing out facts in order to influence people's ideas).

Sometimes this is seen as necessary, for example:

- during a war – to gain civilians' support
- during a period of high security (such as bomb threats) – to make people more aware of a situation.

Sometimes this kind of propaganda can cause fear, which leads to **prejudice** and **discrimination**.

Should the media have social responsibility?

We are all aware that some countries suffer extreme poverty, as the photograph on the facing page shows all too painfully.

Thousands of people die from extreme poverty every day. If it was regularly reported in the news, people might lose interest and become immune to the issue. It is impossible to report a sudden cause or event that began the issue of extreme poverty.

It is often claimed that the media is failing to report the facts. Therefore, people are unaware of the full extent of injustice occurring around the world. This is why many religious believers try to raise people's awareness of injustice.

Activities

3 The two bullet points to the left are examples of propaganda. What others can you think of? Discuss this in a group and make a list.

Activities

4 Look in two different newspapers that report on the same story or event. Try to choose a story that is about some kind of injustice – perhaps someone being jailed or shot for something they didn't do.

  a Are the two accounts different? How? What are the major differences? Why do you think this is?

  b What do you think is the purpose of each article? Explain your answer.

  c Do both accounts use the same photographs? Why do you think they might be the same/different?

5 Read the headline below.

> ## A new start for ten outcasts!

  a First, find and read the passage Luke 17:11–19 in the Bible.

  b Briefly jot down the main facts.

  c Now rewrite the story from two different points of view. You could, perhaps:

  i write the story from the point of view of an enemy of Jesus or a disbeliever

  ii write it from the point of view of someone who supported the work of Jesus and wanted to demonstrate that Jesus was 'socially responsible'.

Must think about!

Think about all the ways that one news story can be reported in the media, for example:

- in a newspaper
- on the TV
- on the radio
- on the Internet
- in a weekly magazine.

Which might have the most influence? Which would you be most likely to believe? Why?

2.7 Prejudice (1)

The next two pages will help you to:

- explore what is meant by 'prejudice' and 'discrimination'
- explain why people are prejudiced and/or when discrimination may occur.

- **Look at these images. What do these people do for a living?**

- **What programmes do they like to watch on TV?**

- **What is their favourite food?**

- **What religion do they belong to?**

What is prejudice?

Prejudice means judging people to be inferior or superior without cause and making judgements without all the facts or the bigger picture. People are prejudiced for many different reasons, including:

- lack of education
- lack of experience
- only wanting to believe one point of view
- only wanting to see the worst in people
- being influenced by other opinions (perhaps of friends or family, or on a TV soap opera).

Religious believers feel it is their duty to be socially responsible and, therefore, not to be prejudiced. Unfair treatment of others can be seen as injustice and is, therefore, unacceptable. Religious believers understand that prejudice can lead to discrimination.

Discrimination means treating people differently because of race, gender, religion or class, or failing to treat people as fellow human beings.

Is the media to blame?

There are many causes of prejudice. Some would argue that one of these is the media, because it is often accused of reinforcing stereotypes. Films and television programmes are designed to entertain people. In order to do this, producers often create characters to fit in with a certain stereotype. Doing this also means that characters will establish themselves quickly during the programme and the audience will form opinions of, and 'relationships' with, a character.

Does the media discriminate?

Some people would argue that the media portrays men in a better light than women. On soap operas and in films, for example, men generally have more exciting 'lead' characters, whereas women play a supporting role. They are usually seen in the role of 'wife' or 'mother', or if they have a job they may be a secretary or a nurse. Men are more likely to be portrayed as business tycoons or the hero who saves the world. Until fairly recently, the majority of newsreaders were male. Voiceovers for adverts and programmes are still more likely to be male voices.

Activities

From Little Britain

1 Look at this photograph. How many other stereotypes can you think of that have been featured on television or in films? Make a list of both the stereotype and the programme.

2 In small groups, compare your lists.
  a What's the group's total number of stereotypes?
  b Did the same stereotype appear in more than one programme?

Activities

3 Working on your own, how many types of prejudice can you think of? Make a list.

4 Complete the spider diagram below on the causes of prejudice.

- A?
- A?
- **What causes prejudice?**
- A?
- Family/Upbringing

5 In pairs, read the sentences below. Which do you think are examples of prejudice? Which are examples of discrimination? Which are neither?

> **WANTED – a qualified mechanic. Must be aged 18–40, male and physically fit.**

> I am sorry; you are not suitable for this job, as your qualifications aren't good enough.

> **Only 2 schoolchildren allowed in the shop at one time.**

> Because you are a woman, you will be paid less than the men in the office.

> I don't like the look of that gang, they must be trouble.

Sacred texts

Stop judging by mere appearances, and make a right judgement.
John 7:24

Whoever does right, whether male or female, and is a believer will be granted a good life.
Qur'an 16:97

All mankind is from Adam and Eve, an Arab has no superiority over a non-Arab, nor a non-Arab has any superiority over black, nor a black has any superiority over white.
Prophet Muhammad's Farewell Sermon (Hadith)

We are what we think. All that we are arises with our thoughts. With our thoughts we make the world.
Dhammapada 1:1–3

Must think about!

Think of a time when you feel you have experienced prejudice and discrimination. What happened? How did it make you feel?

2.8 Prejudice (2)

The next two pages will help you to:

- explore religious attitudes towards prejudice and discrimination
- explain the work of a religious believer who has campaigned against prejudice and discrimination.

- The Bible says we should love our neighbour. But what does this really mean?
- In just one minute, list all the things you can think of.

What do religions teach about prejudice and discrimination?

All religions teach that holding prejudiced views or discriminating against another human being is unacceptable. This may be due to teachings about human dignity and social responsibility. However, many religions also have specific teachings about prejudice and discrimination.

Christianity

Christians follow the example of Jesus, who regularly demonstrated that it is wrong to treat others unfairly because of their sex, beliefs, disability or for any other reason. Below are some examples.

Women

- In the Bible (Luke 10:38–42), Jesus has a religious discussion with Mary. This was unusual, as women were not normally taught about religion.
- In John 4:1–42, Jesus talks to a Samaritan woman at the well. This demonstrates that he did not discriminate against women or Samaritans (the enemy of Jews). Samaritans came from a neighbouring city called Samaria. Samaritans claimed to be descended from Judaism and followed many of the Jewish customs. However, Jews considered Samaritans 'unclean' as they did not worship in the Temple in Jerusalem.

People with disabilities

- Jesus performed many **miracles** in order to heal people with disabilities. He healed a blind man (Mark 8:22–26), and he cured ten men with leprosy (Luke 17:11–19). Lepers were usually sent to live in colonies outside towns to prevent the disease spreading. Jesus proved he did not regard lepers as outcasts.

Race discrimination

- In Luke 10:25–37, Jesus tells the story of the 'The Good Samaritan', in which a Samaritan helped a Jewish man who had been beaten up and left for dead. A priest and a temple assistant (both Jewish) had already ignored the man, but the Samaritan helped him by taking him to an inn to be cared for.
- Samaritans and Jews hated each other. Jews regarded Samaritans as 'unclean'. By telling this story, Jesus is able to explain that we should be kind to everyone, even those who are different from us.

Activities

1 Imagine you are hosting a TV chat show. Your guests are Jesus, the Samaritan woman at the well and a leper.
   a What two questions would you ask each guest?
   b Ask a partner to imagine what the answers might be.

2 Create an ideas map to show how Jesus demonstrated that it is wrong to discriminate.

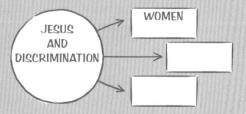

3 Create a diagram to show the similarities and differences between the religious traditions and their teachings on prejudice and discrimination.

Islam

The Prophet Muhammad worked hard to get different tribes to accept each other. He established the *Ummah* (brotherhood of Muslims), which accepts Muslims regardless of sex, colour or social group. The only requirement is that members accept there is only one God and that Muhammad is God's prophet. Muhammad chose Bilal, a black African Muslim, as his first *muezzin* (prayer caller).

Buddhism

The Eightfold Path to Enlightenment states that it is wrong to treat others unfairly. Buddhists believe in:

- right speech (to avoid speaking in a way that will hurt or offend others)
- right action (to act kindly and compassionately towards others).

The Buddha was born a **Hindu**, but rejected the idea of the caste system, which divided people into groups according to social class. The Buddhist idea of *metta* (loving kindness) promotes being kind to all human beings.

The Buddha taught about the law of karma – the idea that what you do now affects your future lives. Buddhists try to treat everyone with kindness in order to gain good karma.

Activities

4 Read the information on Shirin Ebadi. Create a similar fact file for the following people:
- Trevor Huddleston (Christian)
- the Dalai Lama (Buddhist).

How do religious believers overcome discrimination?

There are many examples of religious believers following the teachings of their religion and campaigning against discrimination. Read the following example.

Who?
Shirin Ebadi, born 1947 in Iran. Lawyer, human rights activist and university lecturer.

Religion?
Liberal Muslim.

Does what?
Campaigns peacefully for human rights such as democracy, freedom of religion and speech, and equality between men and women.

How?
Was the first female judge in Iran (1975), but was forced to resign when Iran became an Islamic republic (1979). She continued to practise law and campaign for women's rights.

Conflicts?
Came into conflict with the Iranian government many times and was sent to jail as a result of her campaigns.

Publications and awards?
Has written several books and articles about rights for women and children. Was awarded the 2003 Nobel Peace Prize in recognition of her peaceful protests for equality.

GradeStudio

Question

Explain from one religious tradition how a religious believer has worked for justice.
(6 marks)

This question tests your ability to explain a religious point of view (AO1). Examiners use levels to measure the responses. A good answer will not only make statements about the work of religious believers, it will also explain in detail the actions of the believer and why the believer was inspired to work for justice. There should be clear use of religious language in the answer.

Here is how you might build an answer:

Level 1
First, make a statement about the religious believer and the situation they were trying to improve. For example, if you decide to write about Trevor Huddleston, 'Trevor Huddleston worked in South Africa to try to end racism.'

Level 2
Next, provide a bit more detail about the things the believer actually did to work for justice. For example, 'Trevor organised sports boycotts so that teams from other countries didn't play South African sports teams. He advised other countries not to trade with South Africa to try to stop racism in South Africa.'

Level 3
Then, add more examples of how the religious believer tried to achieve justice. Try to bring in religious words and specialist language. For example, 'Trevor was unhappy about the apartheid system in South Africa, which separated blacks and whites. He became friends with anti-apartheid leaders such as Nelson Mandela. He wrote a book to tell others about the situation in South Africa.'

Level 4
Finally, make sure you have included enough examples of the work of the religious believer. Try to explain *why* the believer felt they should work for justice. For example, 'Trevor was a Christian priest. He felt his religion meant it was his duty to help those in need and follow Jesus' example of concern for those in need. He didn't use violence in his campaigns, as Christianity teaches non-violence.'

2.9 Injustice

The next two pages will help you to:

■ examine what is meant by 'injustice'
■ analyse things that are fair and unfair in the world, and their causes.

What kinds of injustices are there in the world? List six.
Then copy and complete this 'injustice' line by putting them in order of how serious they are
(0 = not very serious; 10 = very serious indeed).

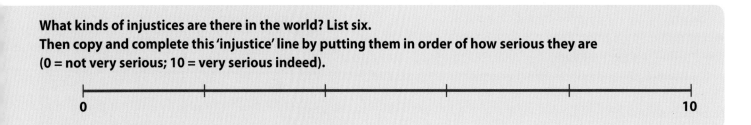

0   10

What is fair?

Injustice means people not being treated with fairness. There are many injustices in the world, which means that some humans do not have their basic rights. But is that fair?

Everyone will have different ideas about what 'fair' actually means. Some people only think about the word 'fair' in relation to their own lives. Are *they* being treated fairly? Are *they* receiving the same as other people they know? But how often do we actually consider whether things in the *world* are really fair?

Here is what many people think fair *should* mean.

■ Everyone has equal rights.
■ People are treated with dignity and respect.
■ There is freedom from oppression.

The word 'justice' is often used when discussing fairness. Sometimes, fairness or unfairness depend on where you are born and grow up. For example, people in many areas of Europe are much more likely to experience 'fairness' than people in less developed countries.

What is unfair?

We often misuse the word 'unfair'. How many times might we have said the following.

It's not fair that my friends get more pocket money than me.

It's not fair that I have to do homework.

The correct meaning of unfair can be summed up with the word 'injustice'.

Activities

1 Create a poster or collage showing things that you think are fair in the world. You might choose:
   ■ being able to travel to different countries
   ■ punishment for people who do wrong.

2 Choose one of your examples and write a short speech to read to the class about why it is 'fair'.

What do religious believers mean by 'injustice'?

For religious believers, injustice means:

- unfair treatment
- treating people with discrimination
- ignoring human rights
- lack of freedom from oppression
- no equality of provision or opportunity.

So are the things that we say are 'unfair' really unfair when we compare them to injustices elsewhere in the world? Remember that, in Britain, our government supports the Declaration of Human Rights (see page 45) and that our laws protect us against injustice.

What is authority? Can 'authority' contribute to injustice?

Authority means power over others through position or moral teaching. Some examples of people who hold authority in society are:

- people with some 'presence' or character
- the person or group who makes decisions
- those responsible for enforcing the laws.

In developed countries, 'authorities' are usually elected fairly by the people. In Britain, adults over the age of 18 can vote for Members of Parliament (MPs) to sit in Parliament. This means that our laws are fairly decided by the people who live in Britain. This is not always the case in other parts of the world.

(see page 45)

Activities

3 In pairs, look at the definitions of injustice on the left.

4 List two examples of when there has been justice in the world (or when things have been fair).

5 Now list two examples of injustice (when things have been unfair). These could be examples from your own life or examples from the news.

A   B   C

6 Working alone, look at photographs **A–C**. For each one, try to decide on the cause of injustice.

Activities

7 As a class, try to think of any times when authority has:

   a been the cause of injustice

   b stopped injustice from happening.

   You can take your examples from current news and affairs, and/or history. A spider diagram like the one below may help.

- Unfair laws
- Ignorance (people ignoring or not wanting to know about the issue)
- **Causes of injustice**
- Unfair governments
- Poverty
- Greed
- Poor climate

Must think about!

Think about the list of 'wants' you made for activity 1a on page 42. Having reached the end of this topic, has anything on your list changed? Can you explain the difference between a 'need' and a 'want'?

on page 42

2 Is it fair?

Remember and Reflect

The questions in this section are based on the work you have done throughout this topic. Try to complete as many as you can.

The questions in set 1 are designed to test your factual recall and AO1 level skills (knowledge and understanding). The page numbers alongside the questions will help you to find information that might be useful for your answers. Use them to check against what you have written.

The questions in set 2 are more challenging, using AO2 level skills (use of evidence and reasoned argument to evaluate personal responses and differing viewpoints). Your answers may come from more than one part of the topic.

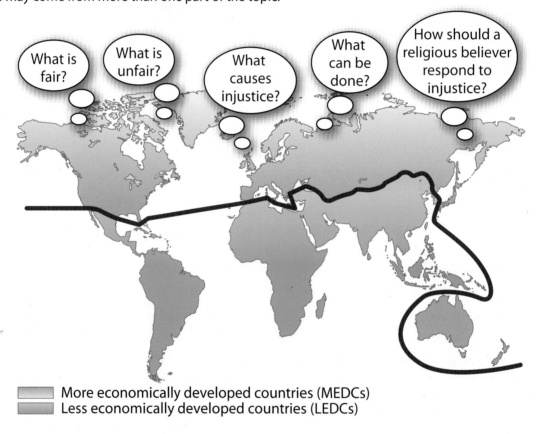

What is fair?

What is unfair?

What causes injustice?

What can be done?

How should a religious believer respond to injustice?

More economically developed countries (MEDCs)
Less economically developed countries (LEDCs)

Set 1 – knowledge and understanding

1	Explain the meanings of the following key words.	**pages 40–41**

    a identity   **b** prejudice   **c** injustice   **d** authority.

2	State three 'wants'.	**pages 42–43**
3	What is the difference between a 'want' and a 'need'?	**page 49**
4	Give two reasons why religious believers believe in 'human dignity'.	**pages 44–45**
5	Give two reasons why people may treat others differently.	**pages 44–45**

6	Give two examples of when there has been inequality in the world.	**pages 46–47**
7	Give two religious teachings about why humans should be treated equally.	**pages 46–47**
8	State two religious traditions that do not agree with gambling.	**pages 48–49**
9	Give three examples of how a religious believer can be 'socially responsible' (try to prevent injustice).	**pages 50–51**
10	Give three reasons why a Christian should be socially responsible.	**pages 50–51**
11	State one biblical quotation that could encourage people to be socially responsible.	**pages 50–51**
12	State two ways in which the media may influence people.	**pages 52–53**
13	Give two reasons why the media would try to influence people.	**pages 52–53**
14	Explain two reasons why people are prejudiced.	**pages 54–55**
15	State three types of prejudice.	**pages 54–55**
16	Choose one religious believer who has tried to overcome injustice. State five key points about their life and work.	**pages 56–57**
17	State three causes of injustice.	**pages 58–59**

Set 2 – use of evidence and personal response

18 Answer the following questions, giving as much detail in your answers as possible.
  a Do you think that it is important to give to charity? Give reasons for your answer.
  b Do you think that rich countries (Britain, USA, etc.) are responsible for the poverty in poorer continents (Africa/Asia, etc.)? Try to consider more than one point of view.
  c Can we ever get rid of prejudice? Give reasons for your answer.

19 'Religious believers should spend more time worshipping god(s) and less time helping others.'
  Choose two religious traditions and try to explain what their response to this statement would be.
  Remember, there may be different opinions within religious traditions.

20 'Men are more important than women.'
  From two religious traditions, explain arguments for and against this statement.

21 As a class, debate this statement:
  'The world is OK as it is. We don't need to try and change things.'

22 'All humans should have equal rights.'
  Do you agree with this statement? Explain your reasons for your opinion.
  Find someone in the class who has a different opinion from you and ask them to explain why.

GradeStudio

On these pages you will find the types of questions you might encounter in your exam, along with sample answers, mark schemes and examiner comments. A good understanding of this information may help you to improve the content and structure of your own answers. It will also help you to understand what the examiner is looking for and how to improve your marks in the exam.

Question

Explain from one religious tradition the teachings about prejudice and discrimination.

(6 mark question, AO1)

This question tests your ability to recall and describe religious teachings about the treatment of others from one religious tradition (AO1). Examiners will use levels to measure the quality of your response. A good answer will not only state a point of view, it will also justify that view in some detail, drawing on religious beliefs and teachings. At the highest level, an answer will also look at the implications of these points of view for society as a whole.

Level 1	A relevant statement of information or explanation, limited in scope.
Level 2	An accurate amount of information or an appropriate explanation of a central teaching, theme or concept.
Level 3	An account or explanation indicating knowledge and understanding of key religious ideas, practices, explanations or concepts.
Level 4	A coherent account or explanation showing awareness of and insight into religious facts, ideas, practices and explanations.

Student's answer

Christians believe that it is wrong to be prejudiced; it is against their teachings. **(Level 1)** This is because Christians follow the example of Jesus who didn't discriminate against people who were different. He was friends with everyone, including women and outcasts. **(Level 2)**

Examiner's comments

This student reached Level 1 by making a relevant statement of information about Christian ideas on prejudice and discrimination.

The student went on to achieve Level 2 by giving an appropriate explanation of a central Christian teaching on discrimination. There is a limited use of specialist language.

To reach Level 3, the student needs to develop their answer to show more detailed knowledge and understanding about Christian teachings on prejudice and discrimination. Their answer should include more examples of teachings about why Christians should not be prejudiced. The student should try to make more use of religious language in their answer.

To reach Level 4, the student should develop their account further by ensuring they have a range of teachings about why Christians should not be prejudiced. The student should use religious teachings and words extensively so that the main teachings about prejudice are fully explained.

Student's improved answer

Christians believe that it is wrong to be prejudiced; it is against their teachings. **(Level 1)**

This is because Christians follow the example of Jesus who didn't discriminate against people who were different. He was friends with everyone, including women and outcasts. **(Level 2)**

Jesus taught about prejudice and discrimination by telling stories like the 'Good Samaritan', which shows that you should be kind to everyone and live in harmony with others. Jesus also taught that you should treat others how you want to be treated yourself, which suggests that you shouldn't discriminate as you would not like it done to you. Jesus thought that we should all live in harmony. **(Level 3)**

Christians also believe that it is wrong to discriminate or to hold prejudiced views as God created humans equally, in his own image. We are told this in Genesis 1. This means that everyone should be respected as we are all God's creation. This is why Christians see it as their duty to treat all people fairly. There are also several biblical quotations that suggest that it is wrong to be prejudiced. For example, John 7:24 states: 'Stop judging by mere appearances.' All of these teachings show that Christians are not allowed to be prejudiced or to discriminate. **(Level 4)**

Question

'It is not my job to be socially responsible.' Give two reasons why a religious believer might agree or disagree with this statement. (4 mark question, AO2)

This question tests your ability to present religious views and explain the reasoning behind them (AO2). In the table, the left-hand column shows what examiners are looking for at the different levels. The right-hand column shows how to build an answer.

Level 1 A simple appropriate justification of a point of view.	First, show you understand the question and state an opinion. For example, 'A religious believer may disagree because there are references to social responsibility in sacred texts.'
Level 2 An expanded justification of one point of view, which includes religious teaching OR two simple points of view.	Next, justify this view by referring to religious teachings. For example, 'In Christianity, the Bible states: "A new commandment I give to you, that you love one another even as I have loved you" (John, 13:34). This shows that we should help the less fortunate. We should show love to others, like Jesus did.'
Level 3 An expanded justification of one point of view, with appropriate example and/or illustration, which includes religious teaching. In addition, a second simple appropriate justification of a point.	Then, offer a deeper explanation of the first point and add a second opinion about the statement. For example, 'A Muslim would also agree because their religion has much to say about the idea of "social responsibility" (or caring for those in need).
Level 4 An expanded justification of two viewpoints, incorporating the religious teaching and moral aspects at issue and their implications for the individual and the rest of society.	Finally, develop the second viewpoint to include a religious teaching to support the viewpoint. For example, 'Muslims would refer to the example of the Prophet Muhammad, who often spoke out against injustice. He encouraged Muslims to help war widows.'

Question

'Humans can never be equal.' Do you agree? Give reasons or evidence for your answer, showing that you have thought of more than one point of view. You must include reference to religious beliefs in your answer. (8 mark question, AO2)

This question tests students' ability to evaluate different ideas about equality and to provide evidence for these ideas (AO2). Examiners will use levels to measure the quality of your response. A good answer will not only describe a point of view, but will also explain it in detail, and will show some awareness of how it links to other religious beliefs and affects the life of a believer. A good answer should also recognise that there may be alternative viewpoints about the issue.

Student's improved answer

I agree because the dispute about equality has been going on for hundreds of years so it isn't going to change. (Level 1)
Women are still treated as the inferior sex even though it is illegal. It is normally men who have the higher positions in the workplace and there are some jobs that are just for men and some that are just for women.

On the other hand, some people might disagree because it is illegal to discriminate in the workplace. All jobs must be advertised for men and women, so really there is already equality. (Level 2)

Christians might agree with the statement because the Roman Catholic Church does not allow women to become priests. They say that, because Jesus only chose male disciples, priests should I be men. A Muslim might agree with the statement because some Muslims believe that Islam is the only way to get to heaven, so religions are not equal. (Level 3)

A Christian might also disagree with the statement because the Bible says that God created all humans in his image, so therefore we are all equal. Also, St Paul said: 'There is no difference between Jew and gentile... man or woman; all are equal through Jesus Christ' (Romans 10:12). This clearly shows that Christians believe there is already equality in the world.

A Muslim might also disagree with the statement because the Qur'an says that God made all humans, so we shouldn't treat people differently because of their sex or class or colour of their skin. (Level 4)

3 Looking for meaning

The Big Picture

- In this topic you will be addressing religious issues about God, life and death.
- This topic covers three principal religions: Christianity, Islam and Hinduism.
- You will need to focus on at least two principal religions.

You will look at:

- reasons for and against belief in God
- a secular society and the value of religion in a secular society
- the nature of God, how God is understood and represented, and how religious believers respond to God
- life after death, and religious beliefs about what happens after death
- religious teachings on death and funerals.

You will also think about the ways in which these beliefs affect the lives and outlook of believers in today's world.

What?

You will:

- develop your knowledge and understanding of key religious beliefs about God, the value of religion, death and life after death
- explain how these beliefs and religious teachings affect how someone might live their life
- make links between these teachings and your own ideas and opinions.

Why?

Because:

- these religious beliefs are reflected in today's society
- understanding religious beliefs and teachings can help you to understand why religious believers think and act in the ways they do
- understanding these beliefs helps you to compare and contrast what others believe, and allows you to explore your own opinions and justify your own beliefs.

How?

By:

- studying and recalling information about religious teachings on these issues
- exploring the importance and value of religion in today's world
- evaluating your own beliefs and views about these issues.

Read these song lyrics.

If God was one of us
by Eric Bazilian

If God had a name, what would it be
And would you call it to his face?
If you were faced with him
In all his glory
What would you ask if you had just
  one question?

What if God was one of us?
Just a slob like one of us
Just a stranger on the bus
Trying to make his way home

If God had a face what would it look like?
And would you want to see
If seeing meant that you would have to believe
In things like heaven and in Jesus and
  the saints and all the prophets

Activities

1 Discuss the ideas the lyrics give about what God is like and what we know about God.

2 In no more than 20 words, write down what you believe is the meaning of life.

3 Draw a picture or symbol that you believe represents the meaning of life.

4 Now debate this statement: 'Life has no meaning; we are all simply following our own paths.'

Develop Your Knowledge

This topic is about looking for meaning. Read the information below, which will help you to think about the issues before you begin more detailed work.

Key information

- Many words and images are used to describe God.
- God is often described as omnibenevolent, omniscient, omnipresent and omnipotent.
- Everyone has their own ideas of what God looks like and what characteristics God has – even if it is to dismiss God's existence.
- Someone who believes in God is called a theist.
- An atheist is someone who doesn't believe in God.
- Agnosticism is when someone isn't sure if God exists or not.
- There are many different reasons given for why someone does or doesn't believe in God; it may be because of personal experience or that they accept other scientific views.
- Religious believers have their own views and teachings about the nature of God and how God should be portrayed.
- God is experienced and revealed to believers in a variety of ways.
- Religious believers respond to God in many different ways.
- Many people today question the value of religion in multicultural and secular societies.
- Religions have specific teachings on what happens after we die.
- Each religion has death rites performed after someone in that faith dies.

Key words

afterlife continuation of human existence after death

agnostic believing that you cannot know whether or not God exists

akhirah life after death in Islam

atheistic believing that there is no God

awe sense of wonder in relation to God's creation or presence

community group of people who are joined together because they share something in common

faith belief in God and religious teachings without proof

God ultimate and supreme power to whom worship is given

immanence closeness of God and God's involvement with the world and human beings

monotheistic believing in one God

omnibenevolence all-loving nature of God

omnipresent everywhere at all times, as God is believed to be

polytheistic believing in many gods

reincarnation process whereby the soul moves to another body or form after death

revelation way in which God chooses to reveal God's nature to people

symbolism representation of an idea through actions or images

theistic believing there is a God and that God is real

transcendent beyond the physical/natural world, outside human understanding, as God is believed to be

trinity Christian belief that there are three persons within one God: Father, Son and Holy Spirit

- Why do some people believe in God?
- Why do some people not believe in a god?
- What is the value of religion in a secular society?
- How do people experience God?
- Why do some people use symbols?
- What influences people's understanding of God?
- How do people respond to God?
- How do religious believers respond to God through vocation?
- How do religious believers respond to God through worship?
- How important is worship?
- How important is a belief in afterlife?
- How important are funeral rites?

For interest

Read this quote by the actress Angelina Jolie. What do you think she is saying?

There's something in people that's spiritual, that's godlike. I don't feel like doing things just because people say things, but I also don't really know if it's better to just not believe in anything, either.

Angelina Jolie

What is the true meaning of life?

Are humans here to be selfish and take what they want or is there some deeper meaning?

If God does exist, does this mean we should be more careful of our actions?

3.1 Belief in God

The next two pages will help you to:

- analyse the concepts of theist, atheist and agnostic
- express reasons for different views of belief in God and explore personal views about God's existence.

- **Have you ever thought about your beliefs about God?**
- **Have you considered the philosophical question of whether God actually exists?**
- **Have you thought about what evidence there is to prove that God exists?**

Why do some people believe in God?

There are many different understandings of **God**. A common one is that God is the ultimate and supreme power in the universe to whom worship should be given. However, it could be argued that, in order to believe in God, there has to be some evidence to prove God exists. Many people – religious and **non-religious** – struggle to answer the question of what evidence proves the existence of God.

To prove God *does* exist, religious people point to:
- evidence contained in holy books
- **religious experiences**
- religious teachings.

Why do some people not believe in a god?

Many people claim that there is no evidence of the existence of a spiritual being known as God.

To prove God *doesn't* exist, non-religious people point to:
- evidence of suffering from the world around us
- scientific evidence.

ATHEIST	AGNOSTIC	THEIST
Someone who does not believe in God and is convinced that God is not real.	Someone who is not sure if God is real and feels that proof of God's existence is beyond human knowledge and experience.	Someone who does believe in God and is convinced that God is real.

Activities

1 Look at the belief line above. Now make your own version. Decide where you would place each of these speech bubbles.

Science explains everything.

How can God exist when there is so much suffering in the world?

I have never seen God, so how can I believe in something I have never experienced?

I was brought up as a Christian and believe that God is revealed through the Bible.

There just isn't enough evidence to make a decision based on valid proof.

I *did* believe, but then a family member died and I couldn't understand why.

A miracle happened to me: my friend was dying but, after we prayed, she got better.

2 Write a paragraph explaining whether you think God exists or not. Give as many reasons as you can to support your opinion.

Activities

3 Copy and complete this table with as many arguments you can think of FOR and AGAINST the existence of God. (You may want to use some of the speech bubbles on the facing page to give you some ideas.)

THE EXISTENCE OF GOD	
Arguments FOR	**Arguments AGAINST**

4 a Look at the statements below. Choose the one that most agrees with your arguments and explain why you think this.

b Now discuss these statements with a partner. Which ones do you agree with? Which ones do you disagree with? Decide on an order, from most convincing to least convincing.

> Science explains how the world got here – there is no need for God. Science deals with facts, while religion deals with something that can't be proved.

> Science explains how we got here but religion explains why we are here. Science is limited to facts rather than being open to the spiritual side of humans.

> God gave humans free will so they could freely choose to do good. We would just be robots otherwise and we would all be the same. God can't intervene in the world, as it compromises our free will.

> Humans have free will, given to them by God, so they can do whatever they want to. That is why God doesn't intervene in the world.

> God has a master plan that humans are not aware of because God is beyond our human understanding.

> God must exist. There are too many examples of miracles and religious experiences for God not to exist. They can't all be coincidences.

> The problem is the huge amount of evil and suffering in the world. Surely if God was all-loving, God would help us.

> Evil and suffering are a test of our faith. Religious believers know that if they trust in God, they will eventually be rewarded.

> Suffering helps humans become stronger. It allows us to deal with events more effectively, so suffering has some purpose in our lives. Without evil, we couldn't appreciate good.

5 On your own, answer this question: *'Belief in God is the most important part of being a religious believer.'* Do you agree? Give reasons or evidence for your answer, showing you have thought about more than one point of view. Include reference to religious beliefs.

GradeStudio

Question

'God must exist because there is so much evidence to prove it.' Give two reasons why a religious believer might agree or disagree with this statement. *(4 marks)*

This question tests your ability to explain a religious point of view (AO2). Examiners will use levels to measure your response. A good answer will explain instead of simply describing why religious believers may hold different views. Try to show how it links to other beliefs.

You could build an answer like this:

Level 1

First, offer a simple explanation of a view. For example, refer to the fact that there are many theists in the world who accept that God exists because they have had a religious experience.

Level 2

Next, develop your answer by giving examples of religious experiences, such as a miracle occurring or people believing they have experienced God through a sacred text.

Level 3

Then ensure you give two separate reasons by showing your understanding of other evidence for the existence of God, such as the fact that science cannot explain everything in our world but religion provides a complete explanation.

Level 4

Finally, ensure that you have given sufficient explanation of your answers. For example, explain that many people are brought up to be theists and, although suffering is a test of faith, it makes humans stronger; God has a plan that humans are not capable of understanding. All these reasons combined are successful evidence that God exists.

Research note

Find out what your friends and family believe about the existence of God.

3.2 Religion in a secular society

The next two pages will help you to:

- explore the question of whether religion has any value in today's society
- determine a personal response to the topic and participate in a debate.

- **Think about the people who live in your neighbourhood.**
- **Now think about your town or larger area, and Britain as a whole.**
- **How would you describe British society today?**

What is the value of religion in a secular society?

Britain today is often viewed as a multicultural society. It can also be described as more of a secular society than it used to be because:

- fewer people attend places of worship on **holy days**
- material needs seem to have overtaken spiritual ones.

This has led to the question: 'What is the value of religion in a secular society?' The answer will clearly vary from person to person. Some might say that, in today's technological age, there is very little need for religion and spiritual ideas. Advances in science and medicine have removed many of the sources of suffering which previously caused people to turn to God. Others might say that religion and spirituality today have taken on different forms and characteristics.

Activities

1 Many people say their interest in religion is declining.
  a What reasons do you think they give for this? Work in groups to compile a list.
  b Do you think interest in religion really is declining? Give reasons for your answer.

2 Look at the list under the subheading 'The value of religion in today's society'. What other points would you include in this list? Now do the same for the list under 'Why religion may not be necessary in today's society'.

Is religion necessary in a secular society?

The value of religion in today's society

- Religion provides stability. It gives a sense of community to those who belong.
- Many of the world's religions have been around for thousands of years.
- Many people are interested in the spiritual aspects of life. They are especially keen on asking questions such as 'What is the purpose of humans?' and 'What is the meaning of life?'. Religion helps to answer these questions.
- You don't have to go to a place of worship to be religious. Many people may consider themselves religious, but practise their faith privately.
- Religion provides guidance and advice on how to act and behave. It promotes good rather than bad values. It encourages many people to stay on the right path and act morally.
- Religion provides support and guidance to people in need.
- Many religious believers help others less fortunate than themselves. Many religious organisations are charities or provide volunteers and help to those who need it.
- Some people return to religion when they are struggling in life and feel they need support.
- Religion provides answers to questions such as 'What is the purpose of humankind?'. Science cannot answer questions like this.

Why religion may not be necessary in today's society

- The importance of a holy day (such as Sunday in Christianity) has been overtaken by the material needs of the world. Shops and other public places often open seven days a week.
- Having morals and acting in a certain way are no longer valid. Crime and drug use are on the increase; many people ignore the rules and ways of religion.
- Many people today don't believe in God. They feel science explains everything for them.
- There are so many religions and they are very different. How do we know which one is 'right'?
- People are more interested in other things, such as going out and having a good time.
- We are a multicultural society and it is more acceptable to do what we want rather than worry about religious ideas.
- Fewer people are brought up to be religious because of the changes to family life in today's society.
- Some religions are promoted in a negative way in the media.
- The extent of evil and suffering in the world makes people question the existence of God and the value of religion.

For debate

Prepare to debate the statement: 'Religion has no value in today's secular society.'

1. In pairs, draw a set of scales similar to the one shown here. Use the points above to list arguments for and against the statement. Add any arguments of your own. Now try to order all your points so the strongest arguments come first.
2. In groups, focus on one side of the argument (you will be told which one). You have ten minutes to prepare your argument.
3. As a class, debate the statement. Listen carefully to the views of others.
4. On your own, write your response to the above statement listing some of the arguments presented that disagree with your view. Include some religious views and beliefs, then sum up in two lines what you have found out.

3.3 The nature of God (1)

The next two pages will help you to:

- explore ways in which God is revealed to religious believers
- evaluate religious believers' experience of God through two case studies.

- **Look at this illustration. What do you think it shows?**

How do people experience God?

Revelation is a term used to describe the ways in which God chooses to reveal God's nature to people. Christians believe that God is revealed to them and experienced by them in many ways. The theme park above shows some of these ways.

Holy books/sacred texts

Religious believers often believe that holy books are sent from God to help guide them through their lives. Some even suggest that they are a direct revelation of God and contain God's words. Often, religious believers feel that God is speaking directly to them and they feel inspired by this.

Natural world

As they look around the world, many religious believers see evidence of God's existence. God is the creator and designer of the world, and some people feel a sense of **awe** and wonder at what God has made.

Religious teachings

Many religious believers experience God through following the teachings of their religion. They get a sense of shared community with others and closeness to God.

Worship and prayer

Religious believers feel that through worship and prayer they develop a direct relationship and communication with God.

Personal experience

Many religious believers have had a personal or religious experience that has completely changed their lives. They feel that, even during hardship, they can put their trust and faith in God.

Great religious leaders

Many religious believers feel that following the example of leaders such as Jesus, Muhammad, Mother Teresa, Martin Luther King and Ghandi can lead them closer to God.

Miracles

These are seen as something wonderful and extraordinary. Many religious believers claim to have experienced miracles and, therefore, the power of God.

What causes people to experience God?

Case study 1: Mary

I was raised a Catholic, like the rest of my family. As a young child I attended church with my parents. My faith was strengthened in my teens when I felt God was reaching out to me. I read his words in the Bible; it was as if he was telling me to help others. Reading the Bible comforts and guides me in my actions. I can't imagine God not being there with me. He listens when I pray and I know I can turn to him for help. I try to lead a good life, as I know one day I will be with God and he will know what I have done.

Case study 2: Sam

My upbringing was secular; my parents weren't religious. I used to get into a lot of trouble at school; I was a bit of a bully and got into fights. At first I thought religion was a load of rubbish. But one day I was walking past a church and it felt like someone was calling me towards it. I went in and immediately felt at peace. I seemed to hear a voice saying that my destiny was to be a Christian. I was a bit scared, to be honest. But I put my trust in my experience and spoke to the vicar. From then on, I was a changed person. I tried to stay out of trouble and lead a good life helping others. My family were worried at first, but as I began to change they gradually supported me in my faith. The walk past the church changed my entire life; I truly believe God called me to him that day.

Activities

4 Read Mary's case study.

   a How does she experience God? Make a list of the things she mentions.

   b How does she know that God exists?

5 Now read Sam's case study.

   a What experience does he talk of?

   b Why do you think his family was worried about him after his experience?

   c What impact did the experience have on Sam? Why do you think this is?

Research note

■ Find out more about the religious experiences of Teresa of Avila, St Francis of Assisi and St John of the Cross.

■ Find out more about the work of Mother Teresa, Martin Luther King and Ghandi.

3.4 The nature of God (2)

The next two pages will help you to:

- explore the nature of God and how people experience God
- analyse and compare your personal ideas of God.

What do these images suggest about God?
Write two sentences about each one explaining the idea portrayed.

What is God like?

Most people have an idea of what God might be like – even if they don't actually believe in God. To describe God, many religious believers use these words:

- **omnipotent** (all-powerful)
- **omniscient** (all-knowledgeable)
- **omnibenevolent** (all-loving)
- **omnipresent** (present everywhere).

God is often described as **transcendent** (beyond human understanding) and yet, at the same time, **immanent** (close to each person and acting in the world). Words such as eternal, perfect, creator and Father are also used to describe God.

God is seen as personal and being able to relate to people. Yet God is also seen as impersonal, a power or force that humans cannot grasp. What seems clear is that:

- everyone has their own ideas of what God is like
- it is difficult to convey or explain God in either words or pictures, as God is beyond human understanding.

Activities

1. Create an ideas map using words and pictures to illustrate the nature of God.

2. Write four sentences that describe for you what God must be like if God exists. Why do you think some people struggle to explain what God is like?

3. In pairs, imagine you are reporters and have been offered the chance to interview God!
   a. List ten questions you would like to ask.
   b. Share your questions with another pair.
   c. As a group try to come up with the answers you think God might give.

4. In pairs, discuss what these quotes say about the nature of God:

> God is not proud. He will have us even though we have shown that we prefer everything else to him.'
>
> C.S. Lewis

> 'I know God will not give me anything I can't handle. I just wish that he didn't trust me so much.'
>
> Mother Teresa

5. Working on your own, think about this statement: 'People's ideas about God never change as they grow up.' Do you agree? Give reasons or evidence for your answer, showing that you have thought about more than one point of view. You must include reference to religious beliefs in your answer.

For debate

Debate each point of view:

> We can never know exactly what God looks like.

> God is revealed to us in many ways, so we know what God is like.

3.5 The existence of God

The next two pages will help you to:

- compare how Christians, Hindus and Muslims describe God
- explain the ways in which different religions represent God.

What do you think this diagram is about?

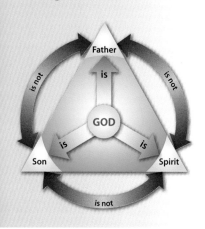

What is symbolism? Why do some people use symbols?

Symbolism means the representation of an idea through actions or images. Christianity is a **monotheistic** religion, which means Christians believe in one god. They use **symbols** and pictures to:

- help them understand and explain God (and the different aspects of God's nature)
- represent Jesus and the religion of Christianity.

Christians believe in an idea known as the Trinity – that is, God has three distinct persons within. In other words, God is seen as one but can be understood in three different ways.

- God as the Father – the creator and sustainer of everything; nothing can exist without God's power
- God as the Son – Jesus Christ came to earth as God in human form to save people and was crucified to redeem the sins of the world
- God as the Holy Spirit – God's love and power in the world today which works to help us.

A good analogy is the idea of water, which can be understood as:

- a solid (ice)
- a liquid (water) and
- a gas (steam).

Although each of these parts is different and distinct, they are all still water.

What influences people's understanding of God?

One thing that might influence people's understanding of God is how God is portrayed. Works of art and films portray God in different ways. Some people view God as being an old man with a white beard; others have a more varied interpretation.

Activities

1 Answer these questions.
   a Why do you think Christians think of God as three persons? Give reasons for your answer.
   b Why do you think the example of water is a good analogy for the Christian idea of the Trinity?

2 a Think of the example of the Trinity in **1(b)** above and draw it as a diagram, explaining how it relates to the Christian idea of the Trinity.
   b Write a short description of how you might explain the Trinity to someone younger than yourself.

How do Hindus understand God?

Hinduism is one of the world's oldest religions. Hindus believe in a Supreme Spirit known as Brahman who can appear and be understood in many different forms. This could be compared to a person who has many qualities, and can be understood and seen in different ways by different people (for example, a friend, a daughter, a sister, a mother).

Hindus believe that Brahman is everywhere yet has no form and can be both male and female. Brahman is seen to control the world through three different aspects, known together as the Trimurti:

- Brahma, the creator
- Vishnu, the preserver
- Shiva, the destroyer.

Hindus generally choose to worship Brahman through just a few of the thousands of deities. They have *murtis* (statues or images) of the gods and goddesses in their homes and in the *mandir* (temple) to help them to focus when praying.

How do Muslims understand God?

Muslims use the name Allah for God. They believe God is beyond human understanding. They accept that God has no body, cannot be seen and is neither male nor female (although Allah is referred to as a 'he').

Belief in the Oneness of Allah is known as *Tawhid*. Muslims believe that the Qur'an (the Islamic holy book) contains the words of Allah. However, they also believe that, because God is transcendent, they cannot fully understand God, so they have 99 names that they believe reveal different ideas about God's nature. Some Muslims believe there are even more names, but these are beyond human knowledge.

Muslims will sometimes use *subhahs* (prayer beads) with 99 beads on them to help focus on the names of Allah when praying. They often use tessellating patterns (interlocking shapes without gaps or overlaps) to represent the idea of Allah being eternal because they believe it is disrespectful to draw God. They think this because no one knows what God looks like, as God is beyond human understanding.

GradeStudio

Question

Explain the Christian understanding of God. *(4 marks)*

This question tests your ability to explain a religious point of view (AO1). Examiners will use levels to measure the quality of your response. A good answer will not only describe a point of view, but also explain it in detail and show some awareness of how it links to other religious beliefs and affects the life of a believer.

You could build an answer like this:

Level 1

First, make sure you show the examiner you understand what the question is asking you. For example, Christianity is a monotheistic religion and believes there is one god who is the creator of everything.

Level 2

Then explain in more detail how God is understood. For example, God is seen as a father figure who guides and supports believers. God is all-powerful and present everywhere, so knows everything.

Level 3

Next, give more explanation of how Christians relate to God. For example, God in Christianity is often understood through the Trinity – that is, understood in three different ways. The Trinity is made up of God the Father, God the Son and God the Holy Spirit. It helps Christians to understand God in these three forms so that they can express how they experience God.

Level 4

Finally, draw together your ideas and show how Christians can understand God through the Trinity. For example, the Trinity shows that God is a spirit with no physical form, as well as Jesus in human form and the Holy Spirit (which is in every person, guiding them). Christians are challenged to understand the transcendent being of God and the Trinity, and ideas such as Creator and Father help them to develop a personal relationship with God.

Must think about!

- Think about the similarities and differences between Christian, Muslim and Hindu ideas of God. Use a Venn diagram to record them.
- Think about this statement: 'Images are the most helpful way of understanding what God is like.' Do you agree? Give reasons for your answer.

3.6 Responses to God

The next two pages will help you to:

- identify ways in which religious believers respond to God
- explore the idea that religious believers dedicate their lives to their religion.

**Look at these two photographs.
Who do you think the people are?
What do you think they are doing?**

How do people respond to God?

People respond to God in many ways.

- They might dedicate their lives completely to their faith by becoming a monk or a nun.
- They might make a financial donation or give up their spare time to help others.
- Some might feel that their religion teaches them to act in a certain way, which they try to follow throughout their lives.

The realisation that God exists can have a significant impact on a religious believer. It can make them change their lives or consider doing things they have not previously done. Here are some ways in which they might respond to belief in God.

Changing lifestyle

They may be more aware of the spiritual presence of God, which could mean a change in lifestyle as they follow the 'rules' of God.

Preaching and teaching

This allows believers to share their knowledge and religion with others. It is a continual process through which others can be informed of God and the tradition being followed.

Pilgrimage

Many religions have special places of pilgrimage at which believers can gain strength and feel closer to God. These places offer believers time to develop a deeper relationship with God, as well as to trace the roots of the religion.

Service and commitment

Many believers try to dedicate parts of their lives to God in service and commitment. They are often prepared to give energy, time and money for their cause.

How do religious believers respond to God through vocation?

Activities

1 Discuss with a partner any other ways that people may respond to God.

Many religious believers feel that they are called to a profession connected to their faith. This may involve becoming a vicar, priest or minister, or a monk or nun. Others may become doctors or nurses, or work with those less fortunate than themselves. Believers with a talent may use it to spread their faith. For example, someone who is a good singer may choose to perform songs to demonstrate their faith to others.

How do religious believers respond to God through worship?

Worship (along with prayer) allows believers to communicate with God. It is a way of developing and expressing faith, and allows believers to come together as a **community**. A community is a group of people who are joined together because they share something in common. Worship can take a variety of forms, including silent prayer, group prayer, singing, dancing, listening, reading and reciting. Most religious traditions have regular sessions of worship.

- Muslims pray five times a day.
- Christians usually pray every day.
- *Puja* for Hindus is a daily experience.

How important is worship?

Worship is very important to all religious believers. It is a form of communication with God and a way they can thank God or ask for something. Worship also helps to bring people together and creates a bond between those of the same faith or believers who hold similar beliefs.

Some religious believers feel that everyday life can get in the way of religion. To regain their religious focus, they might go on a retreat. Many religious traditions offer places where believers can:

- get away from everything
- have time to reflect about themselves and their lives
- have time to reflect on their religious beliefs
- have time to reflect on their relationship with God.

Often, retreats include time to study, read sacred texts, worship, pray and share ideas with others.

Do religious believers need to show generosity?

All world religions emphasise helping others. This can take a variety of forms, such as:

- helping those in a local community
- volunteering to help others in poorer areas of the world.

Religious believers are encouraged to donate money to charity and give what they can to others. Islam supports *zakat*, which means a percentage of a person's income is given to help the poor and needy. Many Christians pay a tithe in the same way.

Research note

Find out how these famous people combine their faiths with their talents:

- Cliff Richard
- Richard Gere
- Yusuf Islam (formerly Cat Stevens).

Activities

2 a Make a list of jobs that could be done to share faith with others.

b Compare your list with a partner. What are the similarities? What are the differences?

A VICAR'S DIARY

To do today...

✓ *Take services*

✓ *Prepare sermon, Bible readings and hymns for Sunday worship*

✓ *Visit the sick*

✓ *Take funeral service*

✓ *Attend meeting about fundraising for church repairs*

✓ *Check list of baptisms and weddings for weekend*

✓ *Attend choir practice*

✓ *Suggest Bible study for Sunday School*

Activities

3 a List the times each day that Muslims pray.

b List the times when Christians might pray.

c In your own words, explain what *puja* means.

(Others in your class may be able to help you with these answers. If not, use books or the Internet.)

4 Imagine you are a journalist. Your editor has asked you to write a newspaper article explaining how religious believers respond to God. Try to write about at least two religions.

3.7 Death and the afterlife

The next two pages will help you to:

- examine sensitively the topic of death and the afterlife
- determine personal beliefs about what happens after we die.

- **Quickly read this verse. In one or two words only, what do you think it is about?**

Do not stand at my grave and weep
by Mary Frye

Do not stand at my grave and weep,
I am not there, I do not sleep.

I am a thousand winds that blow.
I am the diamond glint on snow.
I am the sunlight on ripened grain.
I am the gentle autumn rain.

When you wake in the morning hush,
I am the swift, uplifting rush
Of quiet birds in circling flight.
I am the soft starlight at night.

Do not stand at my grave and weep,
I am not there, I do not sleep.
Do not stand at my grave and cry.
I am not there, I did not die!

How important is a belief in the afterlife?

For many people, the thought of death is very frightening. We all know we will die, yet we do not have answers to questions such as these:

- Is death the end?
- What happens after we die?
- Are heaven and hell real places?

The **afterlife** is very important to many religious believers. It is a reminder that what they do in this life (good or bad) may affect their eternal lives (what happens to them after they die). Some religious believers would argue that reaching the afterlife is their end goal, and they must therefore always be aware of how they live life now.

Activities

1 In pairs, reread the poem above. Explain what you think it says about death.

2 Read these statements about life after death.

   a Write down whether you think they are religious or non-religious ideas.

   b Which statements do you most agree with? Why?

> I believe death is just the end; there is nothing else.

> After death, the soul goes into another body for a new life.

> I think you go to heaven to be with God.

> I think we would all like to believe there is something, but it's just wishful thinking.

> You need to keep an open mind; there is no real evidence either way.

> I believe in heaven and hell. Good people go to heaven; bad people go to hell.

> I don't know, but I don't think death is the end. There must be something else.

> I think there has to be something else after death in order to make sense of this life.

What do Muslims believe about life after death?

Muslims believe that they are responsible for, and will be judged on, their actions on earth. Islam teaches that Muslims have both a physical body and a soul. The soul lives on after death and waits to be judged. *Akhirah* is the Muslim term used for life after death.

Muslims believe that, on the Day of Judgement, they will be judged for their actions in life. They believe the soul is released immediately after death and goes to the Angel of Death to wait for the Day of Judgement. The actions and deeds of each individual are recorded by two angels. The Qur'an teaches that, on the Day of Judgement, the righteous will go to *Jannat* (Paradise) and the unrighteous to *Jahannam* (Hell).

A description of *Jannat* (Paradise)
This is often portrayed as a garden where people will be young again and able to enjoy all its pleasures. Muslims believe that Paradise is so wonderful that no one can truly understand the reward that waits there.

A description of *Jahannam* (Hell)
This is portrayed as a place of intense heat and torture where the fires are never put out. It is a place of great suffering.

Activities

3 Draw a picture of what you think Muslims might believe heaven and hell look like.

4 Imagine you are a Christian, Muslim or Hindu. Write a letter to a friend explaining your beliefs about death and the afterlife. Make sure you explain your views clearly and give reasons for your actions in this life.

What do Hindus believe about life after death?

Hinduism has very distinct teachings about life after death. Hindus accept **reincarnation** – the belief that, after death, the *atman* (soul) of a person passes into a new body and life. This new life depends on how the person lived their previous life. Hindus believe in karma, which is the sum of the good and bad actions taken. Good karma helps with a better rebirth.

As all living creatures are part of the process of reincarnation, Hindus believe it is possible to be reborn as animals, insects or plants. Humans are viewed as the highest form of life, but the ultimate goal of a Hindu is to break the cycle of reincarnation they are in and achieve *Moksha*. When the *atman* is free from the cycle, it is believed that the person returns to be with Brahman.

I am the Resurrection and the Life. Whoever believes in me will live even though he dies; and whoever lives and believes in me will never die.
John 11:25–26

Those who have embraced faith and done good works shall rejoice in a fair garden; but those who have disbelieved… shall be delivered up for punishment.
Qur'an 30:15–16

As a man casts off worn-out garments and puts on new ones, so the embodied soul casts off the worn-out body and enters other new ones.
Bhagavad Gita 2:22

3.8 Funeral and mourning rites: Christian funerals

The next two pages will help you to:

- assess the purpose and importance of Christian funerals
- explain what Christians believe happens to a Christian after they die.

**Look at these two photographs.
Do you recognise the things you can see?**

Activities

1 Create a fact file on Christian funerals.

2 Look again at the photographs at the top of the page. Write a description of what you can see happening in each one. Be as descriptive as possible.

How important are funeral rites?

Funerals are a way of celebrating the life of the deceased; they allow friends and family to say goodbye and grieve for their loved one. A funeral marks the end of a person's life. It allows people to pay their respects and remember the deceased.

Although funerals today can be personalised, there are still many religious features that take place. Funerals can also vary within Christianity, with individuals choosing to follow their own personal traditions and teachings. Sometimes the priest or minister may have visited the person before they died to say prayers or read from the Bible. Last rites (when the priest makes the sign of the cross on the person's forehead) may also be performed. This provides an opportunity for the person to repent of their sins and ask for forgiveness, two very important Christian concepts.

What happens in a Christian funeral service?

- The service often starts with the words from John 11 ('I am the resurrection and the life'), as Christians believe in eternal life after death.
- The deceased will be either buried or cremated depending on their choice or that of their family.
- Poems or a reading from the Bible may be included.
- Hymns will be sung. 'The Lord is my Shepherd' is a popular choice.
- Prayers will be spoken for the deceased on their journey and also for the bereaved family and friends left behind.
- There will be a eulogy – someone will say a few words about the life of the deceased.
- If the body is buried, the words of committal may be said: 'Earth to earth, ashes to ashes, dust to dust; in sure and certain hope of the resurrection to eternal life through our Lord Jesus Christ, who died, was buried and rose again for us. To him be glory forever and ever.'
- Cremation services will have something similar to the above.
- Often friends and family will gather afterwards so they can share memories.

Activities

3 On your own, create an ideas map of all your ideas about Heaven and Hell. Use words and pictures to illustrate your ideas. Look at the ideas above to get you started.

4 Find and read 'The Parable of the Sheep and the Goats' (Matthew 25:31–46).

  a Who are the sheep and who are the goats?

  b Why are the sheep rewarded for their behaviour? Why are the goats punished for theirs?

  c How are Heaven and Hell described in the parable?

  d How might the teachings of this parable be applied to life today? Give examples to show your understanding.

5 Write a short poem, or lyrics for a song, that would be suitable to give to someone who has recently suffered the loss of a loved one.

What happens when we die?

This is a very challenging question, because the answer is: 'We just don't know.' Christians believe in eternal life after death. The resurrection of Jesus, where he was brought back to life by God after being crucified, shows them this. Others without strong beliefs may not have such a clear view. Most people, though, will have some idea of what they think is meant by Heaven, Hell and Purgatory. Many Christians accept that human beings have a soul which is the spiritual part of a person that continues after death. They believe that the soul enters the afterlife.

Heaven
Place of eternal happiness with God.

Hell
State of being separated from God; often portrayed as a fiery place of punishment.

Purgatory
Roman Catholic idea about where the soul goes until it has been purified and can go to Heaven.

Must think about!

- Some people believe that the quickest way to cope with grief and the funeral of a loved one is to try to return to normal life. What do you think? Make a class list of the pros and cons of this idea.

God will wipe away every tear from their eyes. There will be no more death, sadness, crying or pain. All the old ways are gone.

Revelation 21:4

3.9 Funeral and mourning rites: Islam and Hinduism

The next two pages will help you to:

- compare Muslim and Hindu teachings about death and the afterlife
- explore what happens in Islam and Hinduism when someone dies.

Do you think that Muslim, Hindu and Christian funerals are very different? What makes you think this?

A Muslim funeral

What happens when Muslims and Hindus die?

After a person from the Islamic or Hindu community dies, various rituals and traditions are carried out. This happens out of respect for the dead and for the family of the deceased.

Muslim funerals

- The Shahdah should be spoken by the person dying or, if not, by someone else to show the strength of their faith in Islam and Allah.
- When someone is dying the family gathers to say prayers from the Qur'an.
- After death, the body is washed three times by the husband/wife or someone of the same sex as the deceased.
- The body is wrapped in a shroud – often the clothes worn on *Hajj* to Makkah.
- The burial takes place soon after death – within 24 hours if possible.
- Usually only men attend the funeral.
- The Imam leads prayers at the Mosque and at the graveside.
- The body is buried facing Makkah and cremation is forbidden.
- Passages from the Qur'an are recited.
- Many gravestones are very simple.
- Muslims believe that the period of mourning should be kept brief and usually last only three days.

Hindu funerals

- Once a Hindu has died, the immediate family will carry out the rituals needed.
- The body is prepared by putting water from the River Ganges or a *tulsi* leaf in the mouth.
- Time is given for the family to say goodbye.
- The funeral should take place within 24 hours if possible.
- The ceremony is usually led by the priest and eldest son.
- Cremation is preferred; Hindus believe in reincarnation, and it is thought that the *atman* (soul) is released when the body is cremated.
- Only *saddhus* (holy men) and children are buried.
- The ashes are usually scattered in running water, and in the River Ganges if possible.
- The deceased is usually commemorated every year.

Activities

1 Imagine you have a student in your class who knows nothing about Muslim funerals. Design and create a leaflet to explain to them what happens.

A Hindu cremation ceremony

Activities

2 Imagine you are a reporter for your local newspaper. Write a report of the funeral you recently attended of a member of the Hindu community.

3 On your own, complete a Venn diagram showing the main similarities and differences between Hindu and Muslim funerals.

4 A funeral director needs your help to arrange a multi-faith funeral. Think about what you have learned here and on pages 82–83 about death and burial for Christianity, Islam and Hinduism. Then try to advise the person on what aspects of each religion you would use, and why.

Sacred texts

No one dies unless Allah permits. The term of every life is fixed.

Qur'an 3:145

He created life and death in order to test which of you does good works.

Qur'an 67:2

For death is certain to one who is born…thou shalt not grieve for what is unavoidable.

Bhagavad Gita 2:27

From the unreal lead me to the real!
From darkness lead me to light!
From death lead me to immortality!

Brihadaranyaka Upanishad 1.3.28

GradeStudio

Question

Explain the teachings of life after death from two religious traditions. *(6 marks)*

This question tests your ability to explain religious teachings and what religious believers think about life after death (AO1). Examiners will use levels to measure the quality of your response. A good answer will not only describe a point of view, but will also explain it in detail and show some awareness of how it links to other religious beliefs and affects the life of a believer.

You could build an answer like this:

Level 1

First, let the examiner know you understand what the question is asking. Explain that different religions have different teachings about life after death. For example, Christianity believes in heaven and hell, while Hinduism accepts reincarnation, in which the soul moves on to another body.

Level 2

Next, go on to explain these ideas in more depth. For example, describe what Christians believe heaven and hell are like and explain what the idea of reincarnation involves.

Level 3

Then give further information about judgement for Christians and Hindus. For example, Christians believe that life after death is determined by how they live their lives on earth. You could make reference to the 'Parable of the Sheep and the Goats'. Similarly, Hindus believe that their actions will result in a better or worse rebirth. Make sure you give examples.

Level 4

Finally, try to convey that religious teachings about life after death are very important as they affect how a Christian or Hindu may live their lives. They will always be aware of how their actions have consequences, not only in their current life but also for life after death.

3 Looking for meaning
Remember and Reflect

The questions in this section are based on the work you have done throughout this topic. Try to complete as many as you can.

The questions in set 1 are designed to test your factual recall and AO1 level skills (knowledge and understanding). The page numbers alongside the questions will help you to find information that might be useful for your answers. Use them to check against what you have written.

The questions in set 2 are more challenging, using AO2 level skills (use of evidence and reasoned argument to evaluate personal responses and differing viewpoints). Your answers may come from more than one part of the topic.

'DOES GOD EXIST?'

'WHAT IS GOD LIKE?'

'WHAT HAPPENS AFTER WE DIE?'

'WHAT IS GOD LIKE?'

'WHAT VALUE DOES RELIGION HAVE?'

Set 1 – knowledge and understanding

1	Explain what each of the following key words means. Use one sentence for each word.	**pages 66–69**

	a agnostic	**b** awe	**c** atheist
	d theist	**e** monotheism	**f** polytheism

2 Give two reasons why someone might believe in God.

3 Give two reasons why someone might not believe in God.

4	What does it mean to say that Britain today is a more secular society than it used to be?	**pages 70–71**

5	Give two reasons why someone might argue that religion today is declining.	**pages 70–71**

6	Give three reasons why someone might argue that religion is valuable in today's society.	**pages 70–71**

7	Give three ways in which God is revealed to people.	**pages 72–73**

8 Explain how God can be known through:
a the natural world   **b** religious books and sacred texts
c miracles   **d** personal experience.

9	Give five words that a religious believer might use to describe God. Using your own words, explain each idea.	**pages 74–75**

10	Why do religious believers use symbols to help them to understand God?	**pages 76–77**

11	Explain the Christian idea of the Trinity.	**page 76**

12	What is the Hindu idea of the Trimurti?	**page 77**

13 What name do Muslims use for God? **page 77**

14 Muslims have 99 names for God. What is the purpose of these? **page 77**

15 Give three ways in which religious believers can respond to God. **pages 78–79**

16 How might a religious believer dedicate their life to God? **pages 78–79**

17 Why do religious believers think it is important to have a belief in the afterlife? **pages 80–81**

18 Explain what Christians believe about life after death. **pages 80–81**

19 Explain Muslim ideas about the afterlife. **pages 80–81**

20 What do Hindus believe about life after death? **pages 80–81**

21 Why is it important to have funeral rites? **pages 82–83**

22 Explain what happens at a Christian funeral service. (Try to summarise your ideas in a maximum of six bullet points.) **pages 82–83**

23 Give a brief description of the Christian ideas of heaven, hell and purgatory. **pages 82–83**

24 Explain what happens at a Muslim funeral. **pages 84–85**

25 Describe the funeral rites that take place after a Hindu dies. **page 84**

Set 2 – use of evidence and personal response

26 Answer the following questions, giving as much detail as possible.

    a Are you a theist, atheist or agnostic? Give at least three reasons to support your answer.

    b Do you think religion is important in today's society? Explain your answer fully.

    c Do you believe in life after death? Why or why not?

    d Do you think funeral rites are important? Explain why you think this.

27 *'We shouldn't worry about life after death but instead be concerned about the life we are living now.'* Do you agree? Give reasons or evidence for your answer, showing that you have thought of more than one point of view. You must include reference to religious beliefs in your answer. Try to draw a table showing arguments for and against the statement, then complete your answer, making sure you use religious ideas and teachings.

28 Copy and complete the table below to show how a Christian, Muslim and Hindu might respond to the statements. (Remember: not all religious believers agree on everything, so try to reflect this in your answers.) Make sure you include reference to religious knowledge and give as many reasons for each view as possible.

Statement	What would a Christian say and why?	What would a Muslim say and why?	What would a Hindu say and why?
Belief in God is the most important part of being religious.			
Religion is more important in today's more secular society than ever before.			
Belief in life after death is more important than anything else.			
Symbols don't help us to understand God any better than being without them, because God is beyond our understanding.			

GradeStudio

On these pages you will find the types of questions you might encounter in your exam, along with sample answers, mark schemes and examiner comments. A good understanding of this information may help you to improve the content and structure of your own answers. It will also help you to understand what the examiner is looking for and how to improve your marks in the exam.

Question

Explain the funeral rites of two religious traditions. **(6 mark question, AO1)**

This question tests your ability to explain religious teachings and explain what religious believers do when someone dies (AO1). Examiners will use levels to measure the quality of your response. A good answer will not only describe a funeral rite, but will also explain it in detail, and show some awareness of how it links to other religious beliefs and affects the life of a believer.

Level 1	**Level 2**
A relevant statement of information or explanation, limited in scope.	An accurate amount of information or an appropriate explanation of a central teaching, theme or concept.
Level 3	**Level 4**
An account or explanation indicating knowledge and understanding of key religious ideas, practices, explanations or concepts.	A coherent account or explanation showing awareness and insight into religious facts, ideas, practices and explanations.

Student's answer

Christian believe funeral rites are important because they are the last rite of passage for Christians. **(Level 1)** The funeral service itself will usually take place in a church and be led by a minister who reminds those present that Christians believe in Heaven. Afterwards, the deceased person may be buried or cremated. **(Level 2)** Hymns are sung and prayers are said because the funeral service is a church service. Family and friends will wear black as a sign of mourning.

Hindus believe in reincarnation and therefore only accept cremation. The body will be washed beforehand and the funeral takes place within 24 hours because death is a door that must be passed through from birth to birth. The ashes are usually scattered in running water. **(Level 3)**

Examiner's comments

The student provides an accurate amount of knowledge and shows a good understanding of key religious ideas and practices. This response would gain a Level 3, 4 marks.

The Christian explanation is more thorough than the Hindu answer. In order to secure Level 4, the student needs to clarify and be more specific in the details included. Reference to the eulogy as a talk about the life of the deceased person and specific verses spoken during the Christian service, such as John 11, or the committal words ('ashes to ashes, dust to dust', etc.) would show further understanding of the importance of Bible readings to express religious faith. The Hindu response requires a more detailed explanation of, for example, why the body is put in clothes of a particular colour, who attends the funeral and why and why the ashes are put in running water.

Student's improved answer

Christians believe that funeral rites are important. Sometimes, before death, the last rites will be performed by a priest. **(Level 1)** The funeral itself will usually take place in a church and the deceased person may be buried or cremated. **(Level 2)** Often the service will start with words from John 11. Hymns may be sung and prayers said both for the deceased and for the family and friends left behind. **(Level 3)** Someone will give an eulogy where the deceased's life is spoken about. Family and friends will wear black as a sign of mourning. If buried, the words 'Dust to dust, ashes to ashes' will be spoken at the graveside. **(Level 3)**

Hindus believe in reincarnation and therefore only accept cremation and they believe in the idea of reincarnation where the soul is released into another body. The body will be washed beforehand and often a *tulsi* leaf is put in the mouth. **(Level 4)** The funeral takes place quickly, within 24 hours, and is led by the priest and eldest son. The ashes are usually put in running water, often the River Ganges if possible. **(Level 4)**

Question

'God must exist, as there is so much evidence to suggest this.' Give two reasons why a religious believer would agree or disagree with the statement. **(4 mark question, AO2)**

This question tests your ability to present religious views and explain the reasoning behind them (AO2). Examiners will use levels to measure the quality of your response. A good answer will not only state a view, but will also justify that view in detail, drawing on religious beliefs and teachings.

In the table, the left-hand column shows what examiners are looking for at the different levels. The right-hand column shows how to build an answer.

Level 1 A simple appropriate justification of a point of view.	First, show you understand the question and state an opinion. For example, religious believers claim to have personal experiences of God, so accept this as evidence for God's existence.
Level 2 An expanded justification of one point of view, which includes religious teaching OR two simple points of view.	Then justify this view by referring to religious teachings. For example, there are many religious experiences in the Bible. Christians believe that religious experiences are communication with God and evidence of God's involvement in creation. Miracles are often attributed to God and point to God's existence.
Level 3 An expanded justification of one point of view, with appropriate example and/or illustration, which includes religious teaching. In addition, a second simple appropriate justification of a point of view.	Next, offer a deeper explanation. For example, another reason is that believers can 'know' God through holy books and try to understand God's nature. Stories such as the creation story explain how humans came to exist.
Level 4 An expanded justification of two viewpoints, incorporating the religious teaching and moral aspects at issue and their implications for the individual and the rest of society.	Finally, offer a deeper explanation of the viewpoint. For example, some religious believers accept that science can explain many things but believe it cannot fully answer all questions. Religion offers a solution, explaining the purpose of humans and providing understanding to questions that science fails to answer. Religious believers claim that religion provides knowledge and is evidence of God's existence.

4 Our world

The Big Picture

- In this topic you will be addressing religious issues about our world.
- This topic covers three principal religions: Christianity, Judaism and Hinduism.
- You will need to focus on at least two principal religions.

You will look at:

- issues of creation, human beings and the environment
- religious teachings about creation
- the place and purpose of humankind in the world, and ideas about the soul
- religious teachings about stewardship, including how and why animals should be cared for.

You will also think about the ways in which these issues affect the life and outlook of believers in today's world.

What?

You will:

- develop knowledge and understanding of how the universe began and how this affects a religious believer
- consider the purpose of human life and what makes us distinctly human
- consider issues of conservation for the world and look at examples of how the earth's resources are used.

Why?

Because:

- understanding beliefs about how the universe began helps you to compare and contrast what others believe as individuals and faith communities
- these things can help you to understand why a religious believer would think and act in a certain way concerning our world
- you can compare our own views/ideas about the world we live in.

How?

By:

- exploring different religious views of creation
- thinking about your own 'talents', and your role in the world and that of others
- recalling and selecting information about stewardship and its importance to religious believers.

Read these song lyrics.

Earth song
by Michael Jackson

What about sunrise
What about rain
What about all the things
That you said we were to gain…
What about killing fields
Is there a time
What about all the things
That you said was yours and mine…
Did you ever stop to notice
All the blood we've shed before
Did you ever stop to notice
The crying earth the weeping shores?

What have we done to the world
Look what we've done
What about all the peace
That you pledge your only son…
What about flowering fields
Is there a time
What about all the dreams
That you said was yours and mine…
Did you ever stop to notice
All the children dead from war
Did you ever stop to notice
The crying earth the weeping shores?

Activities

1   Spend a few moments alone to read these lyrics. What do
    you think they are about?

2   In groups, make a list of some of the ways people are
    destroying the earth. Which words from the song might
    support the points on your list?

Develop Your Knowledge

This topic is about exploring creation and our place in the world. Read the information below, which will help you to think about the issues before you begin more detailed work.

Key information

- Some Christians and Jews believe God created the world in six days and rested on the seventh.

- The Christian and Jewish account of Creation can be found in Genesis 1 and 2.

- One Hindu tradition says that Brahma was commanded by Vishnu to create the world.

- Some Christians and Jews have a literal view about how the universe began, and some have a non-literal view.

- Christians and Jews believe in the idea of the soul – the part of human nature that is spiritual in form and influences an individual's personality.

- Hindus believe that the *atman* is the indestructible part of us. It is the part of God inside us that moves on to another body after death.

- One talent a religious believer has is to care for the environment and become a good 'steward'.

- Christians and Jews believe animals should be cared for because they are part of God's creation and humans were given a responsibility to care for animals.

- Hindus believe that animals have feelings and that their souls are reincarnated into different life forms over time. Many Hindus are vegetarians.

Key words

anadi Hindu expression for 'beginning-less'

atman the soul in Hinduism, the part of God inside us that moves on to another body or form after death

Big Bang Theory belief that everything started with a big bang about 14 billion years ago; the universe began to expand, then cooled down, forming the earth and other planets

creation way in which something is uniquely made; God's Creation of the universe

dominion being in charge and having power over others

environment surroundings of the place in which human beings live

ex nihilo out of nothing

humanity all the people who live on the earth; a sense of compassion or benevolence towards other members of the human race

literal believing that the creation account as told in the Bible is true – it happened literally as it is described

natural resources substances such as coal and oil that occur naturally and have a valuable purpose for humans and the world today

non-literal believing that the creation account as told in the Bible is not a literal account of how creation occurred

soul part of human nature that is spiritual in form and influences an individual's personality

stewardship God-given responsibility to care for the world

talent something we are good at

Theory of Evolution argument that life began in simple forms and evolved into the more complex forms we see today

universe everything that exists; everything in space and time

Key questions

- How did the universe begin?
- How can we use our talents?
- Why should we use our talents?
- Why are we here?
- What makes us human?
- How should we use natural resources?
- How should animals be treated?
- Why should we care for the world?

For interest

Many works of fiction, TV programmes and films (for example, *Star Wars*, *Red Dwarf*, *Lord of the Rings*, *Hitchhiker's Guide to the Galaxy*) create their own worlds and universes. Some characters in works of fiction are able to inhabit both our world as we know it and other universes/galaxies – for example, Dr Who and the children in *The Chronicles of Narnia*.

In groups, pick an alternative universe/world/galaxy that you know of from fiction. Then try to answer these questions.

- How was this place created?
- Who created it?
- Who lives there?
- How do they live there? In houses? In caves? In spaceships?
- What resources do they have?
- Are those resources being wasted or destroyed? How?
- Do those living there care about their planet? How do they try to protect it?
- Are the issues of this fictional place so very different from the issues in our world today?

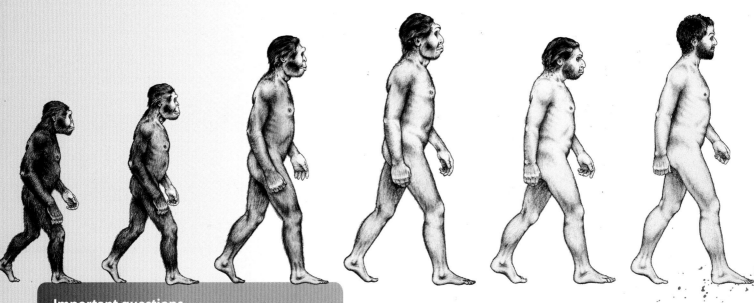

Important questions

- Why does the world need human beings?
- Should we care about how the universe began?
- Should we care about the world today?

4.1 Creation

> **The next two pages will help you to:**
> - explore a range of ideas about the creation of the universe
> - examine the beliefs of religious believers and scientists.

- How do *you* think the universe began?
- What are your reasons for these views?

How did the universe begin?

Several attempts have been made throughout history to answer this question, but no answer has been agreed. Many people believe that the universe is God's **Creation** and that God created the world out of nothing (*ex nihilo*), while others accept a more scientific view of Creation. 'Creation' refers to something being uniquely made. For religious believers this means God created the world out of nothing (*ex nihilo*).

What do Christians and Jews believe?

Christians and Jews traditionally believe that God created the world *ex nihilo* (from nothing) in six days and rested on the seventh. God also created *ex nihilo*: light and darkness; sea and sky; land and plants; sun, moon and stars; all living creatures; and human beings, created in the image of God.

Religious believers have differing views about how God created the world. These views are known as **literalist** and **non-literalist**.

What do Hindus believe?

Hindus believe that everything has existed without *anadi* (a beginning) and that creation is eternal. They believe in cycles of creation. Brahman, the Supreme Spirit, is responsible for this. Brahman comprises three parts:

- Brahma, the creator, who makes the world and all life
- Vishnu, the preserver, who looks after the world
- Shiva, the destroyer, who ends the world so Brahma can make it again.

The Upanishads explain how five elements – ether, air, water, earth and fire – are all sacrificed to renew all life.

The Rig Veda describes how the universe was made from the parts of the first man, Purusha. Four *varnas* (castes) were taken from his body:

- Brahmins (priests) from the mouth
- Kshatriyas (warriors or rulers) from the arms
- Vaisyas (skilled workers and traders) from the thighs
- Sudras (servants and unskilled labourers) from the feet.

Literal view

Christians and Jews who accept this view believe creation literally happened as the Bible states – for example:

- *it took God six days, each of 24 hours, to create the world*
- *Adam (the first man on earth) was formed from the dust of the earth*
- *Eve (the first woman) was formed from Adam's rib.*

Non-literal view

Christians and Jews who accept this view believe that the fact God created the world is more important than how God created it. They also accept that the Bible account is poetic. Therefore:

- *the Bible account is not literal but does state that God created the world*
- *the time of creation was not necessarily in six days lasting 24 hours each.*

> **Activities**
>
> 1 List the similarities and differences between the Christian and Hindu accounts of creation.
>
> 2 Write your own creation myth. Use some of the above or make up your own. Share your story with the rest of the class.

What does science say about creation?

There are two mains teachings that scientists use to explain how the universe and life began.

Big Bang Theory

This states that the world began with a 'big bang' about 14 billion years ago. First, the universe began to expand. Then it cooled down, forming the stars, the Earth and other planets. The universe continues to expand and cool today, just as it did then. This is just a theory, though, and not all scientists believe it. It gives no detail about *why* the world was created. Some Christians accept God as being the cause of the Big Bang.

Theory of Evolution

Charles Darwin (1809–1882) argued that life began in simple forms and evolved into the more complex forms of life we see today. Some Christians and Jews see this as a problem because it rejects the idea of God's divine intervention in the creation process. It also rejects the idea that God created humans in his own image. Some Christians believe that God is behind the process of evolution.

Religion and science ask different questions about the creation of the universe.

Religion asks...
- Why did the world begin?
- Why are we here?
- Why did the world come into existence?

Religion also...
- tries to explain the purpose in things that happen
- explains the value and significance of things that happen
- uses sacred writings as evidence and therefore can be resistant to change.

Science asks...
- How did the world begin?
- Can we explain how the world came to be?

Science also...
- explains how the process of creation took place
- is based on evidence
- can be reviewed or rejected when new information becomes available.

Activities

3 Imagine you are a Christian discussing Creation with scientists. Write the conversation you would have with the scientists about these beliefs. Don't forget, they would put forward their views as well.

4 Think back to your answers to the questions at the top of page 94. Has your view now changed? Why? Why not?

GradeStudio

Question

Explain two different viewpoints that Christians may have about how the earth was made.
(4 marks)

This question asks you to consider two Christian views about creation (AO1). Examiners use levels to measure your responses. A good answer will not only state a view, it will also explain in some detail what it means and will say how it links to other religious beliefs and affects the life of a believer.

You could build an answer like this:

Level 1

First, let the examiner know you understand the question. For example, 'Christians believe God created the world although they have differing views as to how it actually happened.'

Level 2

Next, give more detail of the different views. For example, 'Some Christians believe in a literal view, while other Christians believe in a non-literal view of creation.'

Level 3

Then describe these views in more depth. For example, 'Those who accept the literal view believe that God actually created the world as it says in the Bible – in six days, each comprising 24 hours. Those who accept the non-literal view believe God did create the world, although not necessarily in six days of 24 hours each.'

Level 4

Finally, draw these ideas together. For example, 'While both views accept that God did create the world, the literalist view would see a real conflict between religion and science while the non-literal view would not. A literal view accepts the Bible is literally true – that is, Adam was born out of the dust of the earth and Eve was formed from his rib. The non-literal view believes the Bible is poetic and can be interpreted.'

Research note

- Find out more about the Rig Veda and the Upanishads. What are they? (If you already know, then explain them to someone in your class who doesn't.)
- Find out who Charles Darwin was and how he became interested in his research.

4.2 Using talents

The next two pages will help you to:

- evaluate how we can use our talents
- identify the talents a religious believer may have.

- **What talents do you have? Make a list. Don't be modest!**
- **Now share these with a partner. Are your talents similar or different?**

How can we use our talents?

A 'talent' is something we are good at. We all have talents of one kind or another. Many of them can be used to improve something we already do. For example, a person who is good at a particular sport could develop their talent to succeed at a higher level. Other talents could include helping people – for example, listening carefully to someone's problems without making a judgement is a talent, and so is being able to explain or communicate an idea clearly.

Talents can be as varied as the people who have them. They can be used to:

- entertain people, perhaps on stage as a comedian, through acting or with a musical ability
- help others who are perhaps less fortunate in life
- care for the environment, by perhaps joining an organisation that promotes environmental issues
- teach others about God; this could involve attending a place of worship or praying regularly and encouraging others to do the same
- develop an ability a person already has – for example, a musician practising to improve their skill
- fight against injustice in the world by campaigning for peace and justice in the world.

Activities

1   List the talents these people may have.
    - Religious leader
    - Doctor
    - Teacher
    - Refuse collector
    - Athlete
    - Lead singer of a band
        a Do these people share any talents?
        b Why do you think some of the talents are different?

2   In groups, list all the talents you have identified from activity 1. Which do you think are the most important? Why?

3   Write two paragraphs aimed at non-religious people explaining how a believer might use the talents they have.

Why should we use our talents?

Whatever our talent happens to be, we can use it to help others and show compassion towards them. For example:

- if we are good at listening, we can help friends and family with their problems
- if we are good at organising, we can help an elderly neighbour run some errands
- if we are good at entertaining, we can cheer people up
- if we excel at sport, we can be an inspiration to others to train hard and succeed.

Some would say that using our talents enables us to make the world a better place. This could include caring for the **environment** and encouraging people to live in harmony with others. Our talents may give us a sense of responsibility, as they allow others to trust us.

What is the religious view of talent?

- Christians believe it is their duty from God to use their talents, and to care for others and the environment.
- Hindus believe that using their talents lets them show compassion towards others and helps them to reach *moksha* – the final stage of existence when the *atman* (soul) is freed from the cycle of birth, death and rebirth.
- Jews believe that they should use their talents to thank God for everything they have been provided with – environment, family, health and so on. By using their talents, Jews hope their reward will be in Heaven with God.

For debate

Prepare to debate the statement: 'Other people cannot benefit from your talents. The only person who benefits is you.'

1 Work in groups of either six or nine.
2 Split your group up into three sub-groups:
   - one to prepare reasons why some people might agree with the statement
   - one to prepare reasons why some people might disagree
   - one to act as 'judges'; this group needs to form an overview of both sides of the argument.
3 The judges should now listen to the other two groups present their reasons for and against the argument. Then they should state who has argued the best case and why.

Remember, the groups presenting their arguments should try to include some religious reasons to support them.

Activities

Hindu temple in Lilburn, Georgia, USA, built in 2007.

Jacob Epstein's 'Christ in Majesty' (1957), which can be found in Llandaff Cathedral, Wales.

4 Look at these two images.
   a What things do they have in common?
   b What talents do you think their creators had?
   c How do you think they used their talents?

5 Pick one talent you would like to have.
   a Describe the talent.
   b Explain how the talent could be used to benefit everyone.
   c Select two of the religions covered on these pages. How could your talent be used for both of these? Explain using a poster or drawing, or write your answer as a blog.

4.3 The place of humankind in the world (1)

The next two pages will help you to:

- identify our purpose in life
- explore the purpose in life a religious believer may have.

- **What do you think is your purpose in life? Now read these quotes.**

- **How do you think each person views their purpose in life?**

> *I don't know why we are here, but I'm pretty sure that it is not in order to enjoy ourselves.*
> Ludwig Wittgenstein (1889–1951)

> *We make a living by what we get; we make a life by what we give.*
> Samuel Butler (1835–1902)

> *Life is something that everyone should try at least once.*
> Fran Lebowitz (1950–)

Why are we here?

This is a fundamental or 'ultimate' question, and one that many people may ask on a regular basis. Some may say they are here to enjoy themselves – after all, we only live once. Others may say they are here to live a good life in order to gain a place in the afterlife.

Finding a reason for why we are here depends on who you are and what you believe. Religious believers have clear ideas about the place of humankind in the world.

Christianity

To respect yourself and others.

To become a good steward by protecting the earth and animals.

To marry and have a sexual relationship ('For this reason a man shall leave his father and mother, and be joined to his wife, and the two shall become one flesh', Ephesians 5:31).

To have children ('Be fruitful and multiply', Genesis 1:28).

To work to reduce poverty ('You shall not covet your neighbour's house', Exodus 20:17).

To worship and obey God, and believe in a life after death in Heaven.

Judaism

To respect yourself and others.

To become a good steward by protecting the earth and animals.

To marry ('Therefore a man leaves his father and his mother and cleaves to his wife: and they shall be one flesh', Genesis 2:24).

To have children ('Be fruitful and multiply', Genesis 1:28).

To give one-tenth of their wealth to the poor as *tzedaka* (charity).

To worship and obey God, and believe in a life after death in heaven.

Hinduism

To respect all life; all living things have *atman* (a soul). Hindus believe that when you die your soul is reincarnated or reborn ('The soul is birthless, eternal, imperishable and timeless and is never destroyed when the body is destroyed', Bhagavad Gita 2:20).

To care for the environment.

To maintain peace; Hindus practise *ahimsa* (non-violence).

To 'do the right thing'; Hindus practise *dharma* (moral duty) to others ('Sacrifice, charity and penance purify even the great souls', Bhagavad Gita 18:5).

To marry, have a sexual relationship – known as *kama* (regulated enjoyment) – and have children.

To reach *moksha* – the final stage of existence.

Why does science think we are here?

Science believes we can answer this question through the idea of evolution. We are here because our bodies have evolved over a period of time (rather than being created by God). Science believes our brains, language and use of technology makes us capable of forward planning – a main reason for why we are here. Darwin's theory of natural selection tells us about all forms of life.

Activities

1 **a** In groups, make notes on what each religion believes about why we are here.

   b Compile a large poster or montage that covers all your notes about each religion.

2 On your own, select two of these religions. Does one of them have a better idea than the other of why we are here? Give reasons for your answer.

Activities

3 **a** Look at the reasons why science thinks we are here. Do you agree? Spend a few moments with a partner discussing what you think.

   b Now read this poem. What does it tell you about why God created humans?

4 Focus on one religion and write your own poem, either individually or as a group, which looks at why we are here and our purpose in life.

> *God's Creation*
> by Joyce C. Lock
>
> *However God created you,*
> *He didn't make a mistake.*
> *Adding gifts and talents,*
> *Passion is His to create.*
> *Out of our weakness,*
> *His strength is ours to take…*
> *Multiplying His precious seed,*
> *All for the Kingdom's sake.*

GradeStudio

'The purpose of life is simply to enjoy ourselves now.' Give two reasons why a religious believer might agree or disagree with this statement. *(4 marks)*

This question tests your ability to present a point of view and evaluate it (AO2). Examiners will use levels to measure the quality of your response. A good answer will not only state a point of view, it will also justify that view in some detail, drawing on religious beliefs and teachings.

In the table below, the left-hand column shows what examiners are looking for at the different levels. The right-hand column shows how to build an answer.

Level 1 A simple, appropriate justification of a point of view.	First, show you understand the question and state an opinion. For example, 'There is more to life than this, as God has given us many responsibilities.'
Level 2 An expanded justification of one point of view, which includes religious teaching *or* two simple points of view.	Next, use religious teachings to justify this view. For example, 'The Bible says God made Christians stewards of the world. So it is important not to waste its resources by simply enjoying ourselves.'
Level 3 An expanded justification of one point of view, with appropriate example and/or illustration, which includes religious teaching with a second simple appropriate justification of a point of view.	Then offer a deeper explanation. For example, 'Many Christians devote their lives to God through prayer and worship. This brings about various responsibilities such as church attendance and preparing for the afterlife.'
Level 4 An expanded justification of two viewpoints, incorporating the religious teaching and moral aspects at issue and their implications for the individual and the rest of society.	Finally, give a deeper explanation. For example, 'Religion offers a deeper meaning to life that is often lost during enjoyment. Some people have difficult lives and religion gives them hope. People enjoy themselves but need to think about the future so their lives can be equally fulfilling.'

4.4 The place of humankind in the world (2)

- **What is your definition of a soul?**
- **Do *you* think humans need a soul? Why?**

What makes us human?

At a first glance, this question might prompt us to think of the physical things that make up the human body: limbs, hair, ears, eyes, heart, liver, kidneys, brain and general DNA make-up.

But these things do not make us uniquely human. After all, animals are also made up of these physical components. So what makes us different from animals? In other words, what *really* makes us human? Here are some ideas.

- Humans have a sense of morality, so they know the difference between right and wrong.
- Humans can change the environment in which they live.
- Humans have the ability to learn new languages and use them appropriately.
- Humans can set up economic systems.
- Humans will work to be productive and earn a living.
- Humans search for meaning in life; they can ask 'ultimate questions'.
- Humans use their sense of time to think and plan.

Many people would say humans are also different from animals because they have **souls** and can therefore relate to God. Additionally, they might say that humans were given **dominion** over animals, as the sacred text opposite shows.

Sacred text

Then God said: 'Let us make man in our image, after our likeness; and let them have dominion over the fish of the sea, and over the birds of the air, and over the cattle, and over all the earth, and over every creeping thing that creeps upon the earth.'

Genesis 1:26

Activities

1 What do you think is meant by 'an ultimate question'? In your own words, write a definition.

2 Write down five 'ultimate questions'. Share them with the others in your class.

3 As a class, list the five most popular 'ultimate questions'. Does anyone have answers to these questions?

Does a soul make us human?

A religious person may say there is more to us than the list of physical parts given earlier. They may say:

- humans have free will (they are free to choose how to live and behave, and are responsible for their actions)
- they can show love and compassion – to care for others and form a loving relationship with someone
- they have various experiences that often affect the choices they make in life
- they experience various emotions that affect how they react in situations
- they have minds that help them to think and decide
- they have souls that allow them to relate to God
- they are created in God's image.

Christians, Jews and Hindus believe they are each in possession of a soul. Christians and Jews believe the soul influences their personality and allows them to relate to God. In Hinduism, the soul is known as *atman*. This is the part of God that is within humans, moving to another body after death.

> **Sacred text**
> God created man in his own image, in the image of God he created him; male and female he created them.
> *Genesis 1:27*

GradeStudio

Question

Explain the Christian teaching about the 'soul'. *(6 marks)*

This question asks you to consider what Christians believe about the idea of the soul (AO1). Examiners use levels to measure your responses. A good answer will not only give a view, it will also explain in some detail what it means and will say how it links to other religious beliefs and affects the life of a believer.

You could build an answer like this:

Level 1

First, let the examiner know you understand what the question is about. For example, 'Christians believe they are in possession of a soul, which is the part of human nature that is not just physical.'

Level 2

Next, explain in more detail what the soul actually means for Christians. For example, 'Christians believe the soul is the part of humans that will live on after death.'

Level 3

Then describe these ideas in more detail. For example, 'Christians believe the soul also enables humans to worship and relate to God. It is the part of humans that influences our personalities.'

Level 4

Finally, draw these ideas together. For example, 'The soul is the "image of God" in humans and it is the one thing that separates humans from animals.'

Activities

4 Draw an annotated diagram of the soul from one of the religions covered earlier.

5 A younger student at your school has asked you what makes us human. Using all the information on these pages, give your answer. You can use words, flowcharts, diagrams, drawings or any other means to help you explain.

4.5 The purpose of humankind in the world

The next two pages will help you to:

- examine what is meant by a 'natural resource'
- evaluate religious thinking about why natural resources should be preserved.

What are 'natural resources'?

Where are they?

Point to them on this map of the world.

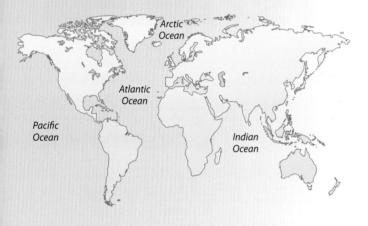

How should we use natural resources?

Natural resources are substances that occur naturally and that have a valuable purpose to humans and the world today. The earth has many different types of resources that are used by humans – for example, oil, coal, rain, wind and the sun.

Natural resources can be renewable or non-renewable.

- Renewable resources can be reused time and time again and will not run out – for example, the sun, the wind and the rain.
- Non-renewable resources cannot be reused and will eventually run out – for example, oil and coal.

Some would argue that it is really important that we use the earth's natural resources wisely. They say that if we continue to waste these resources they will become scarce. When this happens the cost of resources such as oil will increase, as will the products made from them.

We can preserve the earth's natural resources in the following ways:

- ✔ not taking too many fish from the oceans
- ✔ using products that do not contribute to global warming (for example, products free from chlorofluorocarbons, or CFCs)
- ✔ discouraging deforestation
- ✔ encouraging homeowners to use solar-powered energy systems, and to turn off lights and other forms of electricity when not in use
- ✔ saving water by turning off taps and using systems to reuse rainwater where possible (for example, to water vegetables and other plants in the garden)
- ✔ encouraging people to recycle paper, plastic and clothes
- ✔ not wasting food products (by buying only what we need).

Activities

Activities

1   Identify where, within this person's home, they:

   a   would use natural resources

   b   could save natural resources.

2   Look again at the map on page 102. What parts of the world do not have the right natural resources in order to make their lives comfortable? Discuss this question with a partner and make a list of three areas – with reasons.

How do religious believers use natural resources?

What Christians believe

Christians believe that God expects them to look after the earth and all that is in it ('God took Adam and put him in the Garden of Eden to work it and take care of it', Genesis 2:15). They believe that what God put on the earth is a gift, to be used properly for the benefit of everyone, not just for yourself.

What Jews believe

Jews believe that humans need to consider carefully their use of natural resources. After the Great Flood, God promised that the earth would never again be threatened or destroyed by misuse of humans ('As long as the earth endures, seedtime and harvest, cold and heat, summer and winter, day and night will never cease', Genesis 8:22).

What Hindus believe

Hindus believe it is vital that they protect our environment and natural resources. Their belief in *atman* (the soul) means they will return in different forms in different future lives. So it is important that the earth is cared for, and that they should take from it only what they need ('O Goddess Earth ∴ you whose garments are the oceans and whose ornaments are the hills and mountain ranges; please forgive me as I walk on you this day', a Hindu prayer).

Activities

3   Make a note of your own views on using natural resources. Think carefully about these views. Are they similar to any views already covered on these pages? Are those views religious or non-religious?

4   Reread the religious viewpoints. Are there any similarities? Explain your answer.

5   Imagine your school is running a campaign to reduce its use of natural resources.

   a   What reductions do you think it could make?

   b   How could these reductions be supported by religious viewpoints? (You may need to do some extra research on what Christianity, Judaism and Hinduism say about the use of the earth's natural resources.)

   c   Design a web page to support this campaign. The title of the web page should be: 'How my class can make a difference'. Don't forget to include some religious ideas.

Research note

Find out about wars that took place to protect land rich in natural resources such as oil. Were these wars 'holy wars'? (Was there a religious aspect to them?) If so, why do you think that was?

4.6 Stewardship issues

The next two pages will help you to:

- evaluate what religious believers think about stewardship
- investigate examples of stewardship.

■ **What does religious belief matter when it comes to looking after our environment? Surely we all need the earth to live on, whether we believe in God or not?**

THANK YOU GOD FOR LETTING ME USE THE EARTH AS MY HOME AND ALL THAT'S ON IT TO HELP ME SURVIVE

What do Christians believe about stewardship?

Christians believe it is their duty from God to care for the **environment**. Our environment is the place in which we live, but is commonly taken to mean the natural world around us. Christians believe they were given dominion over the world to care for both the environment and animals.

This concept of caring for the environment is known as **stewardship** and is a duty referred to in Genesis 1:26. A Christian can be a good steward by the way they lead their lives (for example, recycling and putting litter in the bin) and through their actions (being kind to others and encouraging peace in the world).

What do Jews believe about stewardship?

Jews also believe it is their duty from God to care for the environment. This duty goes back to the teachings found in Genesis 1:26. The Tenakh tells Jews that God is in charge of the earth, so it is important they take care of it ('For the land is mine; for you are strangers and sojourners with me', Leviticus 25:23).

Sacred texts

Then God said, 'Let us make humankind in our image, according to our likeness; and let them have dominion over the fish of the sea, and over the birds of the air, and over the cattle, and over all the wild animals of the earth, and over every creeping thing that creeps upon the earth.'
Genesis 1:26

For the land is mine; for you are strangers and sojourners with me.
Leviticus 25:23

What do Hindus believe about stewardship?

Hindus believe that the universe and everything in it was created by Brahman. Because of this, they believe it is *dharma* (their duty) to care for the environment. Hindus believe they should maintain the earth's natural balance (rather than waste resources) to thank and repay God for his creation.

Sacred text

For, so sustained by sacrifice, the gods will give you the food of your desire. Whoso enjoys their gift, yet gives nothing, is a thief, no more nor less.
Bhagavad Gita 3:12

Activities

1 Carefully read what Christians, Jews and Hindus believe about stewardship.

2 You have been invited to ask a Christian, a Jew and a Hindu one simple question each about their views on stewardship. Test your questions on a partner. Do they know the answers? If not, research the answers together.

Case study 1: Christian stewardship

Chico Mendes (1944–1988)

Mendes was a Christian steward from Brazil. He began work as a rubber tapper when he was a child.

Mendes believed it was possible to earn an income from the forest without destroying it. In Brazil many trees were being chopped down for furniture and buildings were being put up in their place. Mendes was actively involved with the rubber tappers in fighting against this deforestation. He also organised events to defend people's rights to own land.

As a Christian, Mendes led non-violent campaigns against deforestation by large cattle owners and landowners. From 1985 the rubber tappers proposed to preserve the Amazon forest and create a reserve. By 1988 Chico Mendes' dream became a reality: the cattle ranchers stopped deforesting the area. However, in the same year Mendes was shot dead outside his home.

The land Mendes fought for was named the Chico Mendes Extractive Reserve.

Case study 2: Jewish stewardship

Jewish National Fund

The Jewish National Fund (JNF) is a charity that supports Israel. Its main aim is to supply water and develop the land there. Many fundraising events take place each year in the UK. The money raised provides clean water, plants new trees, provides recycling systems, builds roads and provides housing and healthcare centres. Many Jewish homes in the UK will support the environment by putting money into a blue and white *pushke* (donation box). The money raised has helped to rebuild the Jewish homeland. In fact, today the JNF owns 13 per cent of the land in Israel.

Case study 3: Hindu stewardship

Vrindavan Forest Revival Project

In the 1980s there were many environmental dangers in Vrindavan – the place where the god Krishna is said to have been born. Many trees were being cut down, which had an effect on the environment and animals. Campaigns were organised to stop the logging. Eventually, with the support of the World Wide Fund for Nature, the Vrindavan Forest Revival Project was formed.

The aim of this project is to preserve and develop the forests in Vrindavan. It also aims to provide shelter, put systems in place to retain rainwater and work towards providing a cleaner environment for people to live in. The project ensures new trees are planted, and has developed educational projects to involve the local community.

Activities

3 Reread case study 1 about Chico Mendes, then form into two groups.
- Group 1: put together an argument on behalf of Chico Mendes – reasons for protecting the forest.
- Group 2: put together an argument for the building developers and other users of the trees – reasons for deforesting the land.

4 Reread case studies 2 and 3. Think about their similarities and differences, and represent these in a diagram. You could use a table, a Venn diagram or a spider diagram.

5 Imagine you have been asked to think of a stewardship project. Choose a project for one of the three religions covered earlier.

Then outline these project details:
- what the project will do
- why you have chosen it
- how you think this project would reflect the religious beliefs of its members.

4.7 Animal rights

The next two pages will help you to:

- evaluate why animals are important to humans
- explore religious believers' views on animal rights.

- Look at these two photographs.
- Which animal do you think deserves a good home? Why?

How should animals be treated?

Animals are treated in different ways by different cultures and countries. In the UK, for example, there are organisations on the one hand that campaign for animal rights, and on the other that use animals for experimentation (to improve medicines and other products that humans use). Some cultures keep animals as pets and think they should be treated with respect; others don't think there is any place for animals in the home and see no need to worry about their well-being.

Animals provide a range of things in the Western world, for example:

- companionship (as pets)
- working to help humans (as sheep or police dogs)
- helping to sustain a balanced environment.

Animals are also used for food in most parts of the world.

What do Christians and Jews believe about animal rights?

Christians and Jews believe that it is important to care for animals because they are part of God's creation. Humans were also given the responsibility as stewards to look after animals. Christians and Jews believe that humans should not cause pain to other living things – which includes both animals and humans.

Jewish beliefs about killing and eating animals

- Jews follow *kashrut* (food laws) and will only eat food that is kosher (fit or correct in accordance with those laws).
- Some Jews choose to eat only animals that chew the cud and have cloven hooves (such as cows).
- Some Jews choose to eat animals that have been slaughtered in a certain way with a razor-sharp knife. This is known as *shechitah*. (A professional slaughterer called a *shochet* should do this.)

What do Hindus believe about animal rights?

Hindus believe that it is important to care for animals because:

- they have feelings and souls, and are therefore worthy of respect
- they provide a range of resources (dung for fuel; food such as milk and butter) and they can also help plough the land.

Many Hindu gods – such as Ganesha, the elephant-headed god, and Hanuman, the monkey-headed god – have appeared on earth in the form of an animal.

Hindu beliefs about killing and eating animals

- Many Hindus are vegetarians because they believe in *ahimsa* (non-violence) towards others, including animals.
- The cow is sacred for Hindus. It is treated with great respect.
- Hindus believe that karma (all actions) results in consequences. If a Hindu causes pain or death to an animal they will expect to experience pain in the future.
- When animals die, their souls are reincarnated, which means they move into other life forms.

Why are animals so important?

Animals provide many resources for humans. However, a religious believer accepts that they should be looked after for certain reasons. Animals are part of God's creation and should therefore be treated with respect. The way in which animals are treated is important. For example, Jews can eat certain meat if the animal has certain features and is then killed in a certain way. Most Hindus, however, care for animals because they believe in reincarnation. Christians, Jews and Hindus, though, all believe that it is their duty to care for animals.

Activities

4 Imagine you are interviewing a Jew about their views on animals. Write the interview that might take place.

5 Read this news item. Then list the main points it raises.

> Animal protestors were outraged recently when a sacred Hindu bullock, Shambo, was taken from its owners (Hindu monks living in Wales) and slaughtered. The bullock was suffering from TB (tuberculosis).
>
> Hindus, who were against the slaughter, were angered at the lack of sensitivity to their religious beliefs.
>
> However, farmers insisted that TB in cattle was a major threat not only to animals but also to the livelihood of humans, so it was right to have the animal put down.

6 Using all your notes from activity 5, prepare for a class debate: 'TB is a serious disease. It was therefore right for Shambo to be killed.'

Work in three groups: those who agree with the argument; those against; and those who will take notes on the debate and eventually decide which side has 'won'.

Activities

1 Read the information about religious views of animal rights on pages 106–107 again, then close your textbook. Explain to a partner what one of the religions believes about how animals should be treated. Open your book again. Was your explanation correct?

2 Imagine you have been asked to prepare a meal for a Christian, a Jew and a Hindu. It should be one meal that all three can eat.

  a What are the main religious issues you need to think about?

  b What are the foods you definitely cannot use?

  c Does any of the food you can use need special treatment?

3 Now design a menu for your guests, explaining what you will be serving and why.

Sacred texts

Rule over the fish of the sea and the birds of the air and over every living creature that moves on the ground.

Genesis 1:28

A righteous man pays attention to the needs of his animal.

Proverbs 12:10

You must not use your god-given body for killing god's creatures, whether they are human, animal or whatever.

Yajur Veda 12:32

4.8 Care for the world and the environment (1)

The next two pages will help you to:

- identify why we should care for the world and how some misuse its resources
- examine how religious believers celebrate the world in which they live.

- **Take yourself 200 years into the future. What parts of the environment should you protect now to help you survive in the 2200s?**

Why should we care for the world?

Our universe has been around for a very long time. Humans have been living on earth for about four billion years! During that period, we have had ice ages, land disappearing under the sea, constant increases in population and, in recent times, mass development of our towns and cities. Some of today's hottest topics about our world include global warming, extinction of animals and plants, and why there isn't enough food for everyone on the planet.

Some say we should care for the environment because:

- we have a responsibility to protect its resources and not waste them
- protecting resources will make them last longer
- we will live in a cleaner, safer environment
- we have a religious duty to care for the environment.

How do Christians and Jews care for the world?

Christians and Jews think it is important to care for the environment because it is a responsibility given to them by God. The Bible account of creation in Genesis tells Christians and Jews that God created the world and everything in it in six days and rested on the seventh. God created humans on day six, and put them in charge of the world and all its resources – including animals. This idea is known as *dominion* (being in charge and having power over others). By carrying out this duty, Christians and Jews feel they are obeying God.

Christians and Jews try to thank God for the world he created. This often takes place during harvest festivals for Christians and the festival of Sukkot for Jews. By celebrating and worshipping, Christians and Jews feel they are thanking God for his creation. It also gives them a sense of feeling closer to God.

Activities

1 Look at the list of reasons why we should care for the environment. Which reasons do you think are religious? Why?

Sacred text

Rule over the fish of the sea and the birds of the air and over every living creature that moves on the ground.

Genesis 1:28

How do Hindus care for the world?

Hindus consider it important to care for the environment. They have great respect for trees because they are considered to have *atman* (a soul). The teachings of karma (actions) tells Hindus that the more the earth's resources are wasted, the fewer resources become available. Hindus believe life is controlled by a system of cause and effect, action and reaction. The way a person acts now can have an effect on the future. Therefore the way a Hindu treats the planet can affect what he or she is reincarnated as. For example, polluting the environment and destroying the Earth's natural resources can cause 'bad karma' and affect a Hindu's future rebirth. Treating the environment with respect and various acts of religious devotion (such as *puja*) can wipe out the effects of bad karma. Hindus believe that they should therefore be careful with the resources they use. By obeying God's laws Hindus feel they are able to thank God for all that has been provided for them on earth.

How do people misuse the Earth's resources?

Some people show little respect for the Earth and its resources. They often misuse the earth in the following ways.

- Many people throw litter on the floor instead of using bins provided.
- They waste natural resources such as electricity and water.
- Emissions are pumped into the Earth's atmosphere each day.
- Over-fishing in our oceans means that many types of fish are on the verge of extinction.
- Deforestation takes place regularly, destroying nature's habitation.
- Chemicals are dumped into the oceans.
- Our carbon footprint increases each time we use cars and planes.
- Exhaust fumes pollute the Earth's atmosphere.
- Governments encourage the manufacturing of nuclear weapons.
- Waste is dumped into landfill sites.

It is therefore important that we care for the environment – not just for today but for our future. Many feel that our natural resources will one day disappear if we do not treat the Earth with more respect now. They believe we have a duty to care for the environment, and that people should work together to become better stewards – whether they have a religious belief or not. This will help to ensure future generations are cared for.

Activities

2 Compare and contrast two different religions to establish why their followers think they should care for the environment. You can present your answer as a table, an annotated drawing, or a written article.

Sacred text

This universe is the creation of Supreme Power meant for the benefit of all… Let not the other species encroach upon the other's rights.

Isavasya Upanishad

Activities

3 Imagine you have been asked to organise a multi-faith event in your neighbourhood to celebrate the Earth and its resources.
  - What kind of event would work best?
  - How would you make sure that the Christians, Jews and Hindus in your neighbourhood are all represented in the celebrations?
  - In your celebrations, should you also warn people what might happen if they don't care for the world we live in? Why? Why not?

4 Now write 100 words to publicise the event on a poster. Look for a suitable image you could use. It can be a photograph, a cartoon or something you have drawn yourself.

Research note

- Find out when the religious celebrations of harvest (Christianity) and Sukkot (Judaism) take place.
- Find out how and why religious believers celebrate these festivals.

4.9 Care for the world and the environment (2)

The next two pages will help you to:

- analyse the actions religious believers have taken to help care for the environment
- explore whether religious festivals encourage stewardship.

- **What is happening in this photograph?**
- **Why do you think trees are important to the environment? Make a list.**
- **Now make a list of other things important to the environment.**

What actions have religious believers taken to help care for the environment?

Looking after the environment is no easy task. It's a big world out there, and it is true to say that not everyone cares what happens to it. However, there are many committed people who want to ensure that future generations can still take all they need from the earth. Christians, Jews and Hindus alike all work to support the environment, as the following examples show.

Christianity

Christian Ecology Link: CEL was developed in 1981. It supports Christians from all backgrounds and traditions and teaches that we are all responsible for the way in which we treat the environment. CEL allows members to understand and relate these responsibilities to their faith. Members are encouraged to speak at their local church about environmental issues.

Christian Aid: This organisation was formed after the Second World War to help those who had lost everything as a result of war. These days, it strives to reduce poverty and help people who have been affected by issues such as climate change and famine.

Judaism

The Noah Project: This project began in 1997. It is Britain's only Jewish ecological group and promotes 'education, celebration and action' for the environment within the Jewish community. It works with communities, encouraging environmental responsibilities through festivals and action projects. It also coordinates projects and political action to promote caring for the environment.

Hinduism

Mokshda: This not-for-profit organisation is based in New Delhi, India. It campaigns for an environmental approach to Hindu cremation. Its aim is that Hindus continue their tradition of cremation after death, but that this should happen using less wood and better air flow, which improves combustion. Hindus consider cremation vital so that the soul can be freed from this body and make its journey into the next one. But the current system of cremation uses too much wood, pumps carbon dioxide into the atmosphere and can pollute the water in which the cremated body is put.

Do religious festivals encourage stewardship?

Tu B'Shevat

One Jewish festival that reinforces the idea of stewardship is Tu B'Shevat. This is also known as the New Year for Trees and takes place around January/February. This festival marks the time when the rainy season in Israel ends and the trees begin to produce new fruits. Jews celebrate this festival by eating many different kinds of fruit and also by planting new trees.

Interfaith Creation Festival

In 2007, Jews and Christians (among others) were brought together in a festival to highlight the endangered earth. Each religion talked about how it could take care of the earth in a loving and responsible way. Faith leaders said there was a need to take action on environmental stewardship, which they described as 'the greatest moral challenge of our time'.

Durga Puja Festival

In India in 2006, this annual Hindu festival decided to become environmentally friendly. Generally, this colourful five-day event involves many different kinds of chemical pollutants in all the paints and idols used during the celebrations. So the idea was to use different materials to lower the pollution and other damage to the environment.

Activities

1   With a partner, discuss the work of these religious organisations.

    a   Which one do you think is the most useful?

    b   Which is the least useful?

    Remember, there are no right answers to this question, but you must be able to give good reasons for your answers.

2   Choose one of the religions above.

    a   Look through this whole topic making notes about that religion.

    b   Invent your own organisation to support this religion. What would it do? What parts of the religion would it support? Why?

    c   Find someone else in your class who has chosen the same religion. What organisation did they invent? Talk about the ideas you both had.

Activities

3   Imagine you have been asked to start a campaign about 'Our world'. This campaign should bring awareness to helping the earth survive into the future. The idea is to get as much support as possible from your classmates.

    a   Work in three groups, each choosing a different religion from this topic. One person in the group writes down one way that religion looks after the world. It could be a religious text, or the work of a person or organisation.

    b   Now pass the 'campaign' to another student in the group to add another fact, and so on.

4   When you have all added something to the campaign, compare your document with the other two groups.

    a   What similarities are there? What differences?

    b   What can you conclude about how religious believers have looked after, and continue to look after, our world?

Research note

Find out more about any two of the religious organisations or festivals mentioned on these two pages.

4 Our world

Remember and Reflect

The questions in this section are based on the work you have done throughout this topic. Try to complete as many as you can.

The questions in set 1 are designed to test your factual recall and AO1 level skills (knowledge and understanding). The page numbers alongside the questions will help you to find information that might be useful for your answers. Use them to check against what you have written.

The questions in set 2 are more challenging, using AO2 level skills (use of evidence and reasoned argument to evaluate personal responses and differing viewpoints). Your answers may come from more than one part of the topic.

Set 1 – knowledge and understanding

1 What is meant by the following terms.		**page 92**

   a creation   **b** humanity   **c** stewardship

   d soul   **e** environment   **f** dominion

2 List two problems that exist between the religious and scientific views of creation.	**pages 94–95**
3 What do scientists mean by the Big Bang?	**page 94**
4 Why might some Christians accept the Big Bang Theory?	**page 94**
5 Why might some Christians and Jews reject Charles Darwin's Theory of Evolution?	**page 94**
6 List three things God created *ex nihilo* (from nothing).	**page 94**
7 According to Christians and Jews, how many days did God take to create the world?	**page 94**

8	In Hinduism, what does the Rig Veda say about how the universe was created?	page 94
9	Explain the difference between the literalist and non-literalist views of creation.	page 94
10	State three talents people may have.	page 96
11	Give two reasons why a religious believer should use their talents.	page 97
12	List two purposes Christians have in life.	page 98
13	Explain what Hindus mean by the teaching of *ahimsa*.	page 98
14	How does the scientific view of Creation differ from that of the religious view?	page 99
15	List three things a religious believer would say makes us human.	page 100
16	What does Genesis 1:26 tell us about 'dominion'?	page 100
17	What do Hindus mean by *atman*?	page 101
18	Give three ways we should use natural resources.	page 102
19	What responsibilities do Christians, Jews and Hindus have in the world.	page 104
20	Summarise the work of one steward (for example, Chico Mendes, Jewish National Fund, Vrindavan Forest Revival Project).	page 105
21	Explain why religious believers consider it important to care for animals.	pages 106–107
22	List two ways in which some people misuse the Earth's resources.	page 108
23	Give two reasons why some religious believers consider it important to care for the world.	pages 110–111

Set 2 – use of evidence and personal response

24 'Religious teachings about the beginning of the universe have no relevance today.' Do you agree? Give reasons or evidence for your answer, showing you have considered more than one point of view.

25 'Human beings are more than just bodies.' Do you agree? Give reasons or evidence for your answer, showing you have considered more than one point of view.

26 'Stewardship is a waste of time. One person alone cannot make a difference.' Do you agree? Give reasons or evidence for your answer, showing you have considered more than one point of view.

27 Imagine you are Chico Mendes. Prepare a campaign speech to be heard among the people of Brazil. Describe the current situation in Brazil and give reasons for your work and beliefs.

28 Prepare a list of criteria to judge the qualities of a good steward. Include between five and eight points.

29 Look at the following sets of words and circle the odd one out on each occasion.

e.g. SHRINE   MANDIR   TEMPLE   PUJA

The odd one out is PUJA, as the other three are places where Hindus can worship.

SET A	God's image	Soul	Ears	Experiences
SET B	Replace	Ex nihilo	Creation	Unique
SET C	Respect	Steward	Marry	Pollute
SET D	Misuse	Environment	Dominion	Responsibility
SET E	Literal	Six days	True	Poetic
SET F	Emotion	Spiritual	Human nature	Personality

GradeStudio

On these pages you will find the types of questions you might encounter in your exam, along with sample answers, mark schemes and examiner comments. A good understanding of this information may help you to improve the content and structure of your own answers. It will also help you to understand what the examiner is looking for and how to improve your marks in the exam.

Question

Explain the teaching about animal rights from one religious tradition. (6 mark question, AO1)

This question asks you to explain one religious view about animal rights (AO1). Examiners will use levels to measure the quality of your response. A good answer will not only give a point of view, but will also explain it in detail and show some awareness of how it links to other religious beliefs and affects the life of a believer. You will also be expected to use religious terminology and show you understand what it means.

Level 1	**Level 2**
A relevant statement of information or explanation, which is limited in scope.	An accurate amount of information or an appropriate explanation of a central teaching, theme or concept.
Level 3	**Level 4**
An account or explanation indicating knowledge and understanding of key religious ideas, practices, explanations or concepts.	A coherent account or explanation showing awareness and insight into religious facts, ideas, practices and explanations.

Student's answer

Hindus believe in reincarnation and therefore animals should be treated with respect. (Level 1) Some Hindus are vegetarians because they believe in non-violence towards animals. (Level 2) Non-violence in Hinduism is known as *ahimsa*. Because the cow is a sacred animal for Hindus it must therefore be treated with respect. (Level 3)

Examiner's comments

> This student has given a thorough account, showing knowledge and understanding of one religion. This response would gain Level 3, 4 marks.
> To achieve a Level 4, the student could develop the answer by explaining the Hindu beliefs that animals have *atman* (a soul) and that many Hindu gods have appeared on earth in the form of an animal. The student could also develop their understanding of reincarnation.

Student's improved answer

Hindus believe in reincarnation and therefore animals should be treated with respect. (Level 1) Some Hindus are vegetarians because they believe in non-violence towards animals. (Level 2) Non-violence in Hinduism is known as *ahimsa*.

Because the cow is a sacred animal for Hindus it must therefore be treated with respect. (Level 3) Another reason why Hindus treat animals with respect is because Hindus believe animals are in possession of *atman* (a soul). Many Hindu gods have also appeared on earth in the form of an animal. These include Ganesha, the elephant god, and Hanuman, the monkey god.

Hindus also believe in reincarnation and therefore treat animals with respect. Because animals have a soul Hindus believe that when they die their soul could be reincarnated into another living being and so it is important that all life is respected. (Level 4)

Question

'Humans are more than just bodies.' Do you agree? Give reasons or evidence for your answer, showing that you have thought of more than one point of view. You must include reference to religious beliefs in your answer. (8 mark question, AO2)

This question tests your ability to present more than one point of view and to evaluate them (AO2). Examiners will use levels to measure the quality of your response. A good answer will not only state a point of view, it will also justify that view in some detail, drawing on religious beliefs and teachings. At the highest level, an answer will also look at the implications of these points of view for society as a whole.

Student's answer

I agree with the statement because humans were created in God's image. Because they were created in God's image they have souls. (Level 1)

On the other hand, some people might disagree because when we die our bodies cease to exist – therefore each person's body is like a shell. (Level 2)

Examiner's comments

This student gave a clear opinion and reason for their view, earning Level 1. This was backed up with good examples to support the answer and referred to another point of view, which earned Level 2. However, it is a weak Level 2. To achieve a higher Level 2 the student needs to develop the points made about the soul and the body ceasing to exist.

To reach Level 3 the student needs to write in more detail about both points of view. The student must ensure they include religious ideas about the statement.

To achieve a Level 4 the student needs to use religious terminology and again include reasons for and against the statement. They also need to include religious and moral issues, showing an understanding for the individual or society.

Student's improved answer

I agree with the statement because humans were created in God's image. Because they were created in God's image they have souls. (Level 1) The soul is the part of human nature that allows a person to relate to God.

On the other hand, some people might disagree because when we die our bodies cease to exist – therefore each person's body is like a shell and nothing else. (Level 2) We have no evidence to prove our bodies are anything but this.

Those who agree with the statement may also argue that we were given free will by God. This allows us to decide how to live and behave. This unique attribute shows we are more than just bodies. As humans we also have emotions and can show love and compassion towards others. This makes us more than just bodies.

Other people may disagree as we use our bodily functions every day and we simply follow our instincts, making us just bodies. Showing love and compassion is simply an attribute we develop through life. Free will does not prove we are just bodies. (Level 3)

A Christian may also argue that, as humans were created in the image of God, we are unique and our bodies should not be destroyed. We have minds that enable us to think and decide about various situations. We also learn from our experiences in life. Some people have had 'out-of-body' experiences. These prove to some people that our bodies move on to another place after death and therefore our bodies are more than just shells.

However, those who disagree may argue that we do not actually 'know' that we have a soul or that religion is true. Therefore we can only be 'just bodies'. They may also argue that the 'out-of-body' experiences are often caused when people are ill and have taken medication and could therefore be part of their imagination. Some would say this provides them with evidence to say there is no afterlife. (Level 4)

ExamCafé

The examination is getting closer and it's time to think about revision. Preparation is the key to success and Exam Café is here to help you succeed! It will remind you of key ideas, refresh your memory of what you need to know and ensure that you are fully prepared for the examination.

In order to do well in this course, ensure that you understand the information thoroughly, know the style of examination questions, and are able to present, explain and evaluate information clearly. In the next few pages you will find useful information covering:

- the examination (pages 116–117)
- tools and tips (page 118)
- what the examiner says (page 119)
- how to revise (pages 120–123).

Note
Think positive – examiners are looking for you to show what you can do, not what you can't!

The examination

Here you will find advice on what the examination involves, the style of examination questions you can expect and what you need to remember in the examination.

What the examination involves

The examination lasts 1 hour 45 minutes. It has four sections – one on each of these topics:

- Relationships (Topic 1)
- Is it fair? (Topic 2)
- Looking for meaning (Topic 3)
- Our world (Topic 4).

At the beginning of each section is a page of visual stimuli.
Don't forget to look carefully at these, as they are there to help you.

When answering questions, you will be asked to demonstrate your understanding of:

EITHER Christianity and one other principal religion

OR a Christian tradition within the broader context of Christianity.

Note
AO1 = describe, explain and analyse, using knowledge and understanding.

AO2 = use evidence and reasoned argument to express and evaluate personal responses, informed insights and differing viewpoints.

Examiners will test you in two ways, using Assessment Objectives (AO) 1 and 2. You must show connections between AO1 and AO2. They are both weighted equally in the examination (50 per cent each), so it is important you share your time and attention between each assessment.

Style of examination questions

The questions have five sections (**a–e**), with a set number of marks available for each. These marks get higher as you progress through each topic, reflecting the difficulty of each question and the complexity of skills you are required to use.

Examiners use level descriptor grids (see pages 10–11) to measure your response to each question. Look carefully at these to remind yourself how the marks are allocated.

Each question has similarities, so read the following information carefully to understand how many marks are available and how you should answer each question.

a These questions always ask you to explain a key term. They are worth 2 marks.

Example: *Explain what religious believers mean by* _____ .

b These questions require you to show a link between an idea and how this may make a religious believer act. They are worth 4 marks.

Example: *Explain how a religious believer might* _____ .

c These questions ask you to give reasons for a religious view. They are worth 4 marks.

Example: *Give two reasons why a religious believer might agree or disagree with the statement* _____ .

d These questions require you to explain a key religious idea from two different religious traditions. They are worth 6 marks.

Example: *Explain from two religious traditions the teaching on* _____ .

e These questions challenge you to agree or not with a given statement and provide sufficient reasons or evidence for your opinion. You are also required to demonstrate your understanding of more than one point of view, and use religious beliefs and teachings in your answer. They are worth 8 marks.

Example: *'Statement.' Do you agree? Give reasons or evidence for your answer, showing that you have thought about more than one point of view. You must include reference to religious beliefs in your answer.*

Note

Candidates are awarded marks for Quality of Written Communication (QWC). This includes:
- legibility of writing, accuracy of spelling, punctuation and grammar, and clarity of meaning
- appropriate style of writing for the question
- organisation of material and use of specialist vocabulary.

The 'e' questions of each topic are considered in order to award these marks.

What you need to remember in the examination

Each question has a 'trigger' word to help you identify the style of question. These are explained in the table below.

Question language	Meaning
'Sex is special so should always be kept within marriage.' **Give** *two reasons why a religious believer might agree or disagree with the statement.* (4 marks)	**Give** asks you to describe or state basic pieces of information or reasons for something. Make sure you are clear and concise in your response
Explain *from two different religious traditions the teachings about creation.* (6 marks)	**Explain** asks you to do more than simply describe. It requires some comment on facts or beliefs you describe. Don't just list ideas; try to discuss the points you make and give examples to show your understanding.
'A belief in the afterlife is the most important religious belief.' **Do you agree?** *Give reasons for your answer showing you have thought about more than one point of view. You must include reference to religious beliefs in your answer.* (8 marks)	**Do you agree?** uses evaluation skills and requires you to consider a statement and present differing points of view. Make sure you provide: • your opinion with reasons • alternative views with supporting evidence • reference to religious beliefs and teachings • awareness of how someone's beliefs may affect their view and actions on an issue.

Your final mark depends solely on your performance in the examination, so it is crucial that you understand the format of the paper and the style of questions. Knowing what examiners want is vital to success. Remember, when answering questions:

■ read each question carefully (what information is it asking you to focus on?)

■ look at how many marks are available (what were the level descriptors?)

■ note the 'trigger' word that explains how you should answer the question (what is the question asking you to do?).

Remember, good preparation will build your confidence. Above all, don't panic! Keep reading this section for more tips and advice...

ExamCafé

Tools and tips

This section will give you advice on how to plan your revision, learn the information thoroughly, and avoid the common mistakes and errors made in examinations.

Planning your revision

It is important you have a clear understanding of the topics you have studied. This means knowing and being able to explain fully key words and ideas, which in turn means there is basic factual learning to be done! Here are some questions to get you thinking.

This will help you to structure your revision and cover all the topics thoroughly.

☐ Have I created a realistic timetable for my revision that I will stick to?

Ensure you are sitting somewhere where you can concentrate without distractions.

☐ Will the conditions around me help me to revise, rather than distract me?

You will need these in case you want to check anything.

☐ Are all my notes and materials close by?

When you have done some revision have a break, then return to it and see how much you can remember.

☐ Am I regularly going through the information I need to learn?

Resting your brain is important and will give you time to process the information you have revised!

☐ Am I taking regular breaks?

Methods of revising

- Use revision note cards/memory cards. Use pictures and words to help prompt key ideas.
- Use large concept maps of ideas. Stick them up where you will regularly see the information.
- Colour-code your notes. This helps to identify key words/ideas.
- Ask someone to test you. Checking your learning is very important.
- Repeat information aloud to yourself. Saying things aloud sometimes helps us to remember things.
- Record your notes in an appropriate format (e.g. MP3) so that you can play them back regularly on your PC, phone or MP3 player.
- Use the Internet for background information. There is plenty of help available.
- Use the CD-ROM exam help. This will focus your revision.
- Write out some practice questions and test yourself. Use the level descriptors (pages 10–11) to check and mark your answers.
- Practise examination-style questions. Try to identify where your answers can be improved, and provide yourself with a checklist of information to include.

Note
We all learn things differently, so find a revision technique that suits you. There are plenty to choose from!

Avoiding common mistakes and errors

You are more likely to avoid making common mistakes and errors if you know what they are in the first place! This list gives a typical selection.

Misreading the question. Many candidates misread questions or fail to read them thoroughly. So they answer the question they *think* has been asked rather than the one that has actually been asked. Candidates recognise a key word and fail to answer the question in context.

Giving simple descriptions without full explanations. Candidates often fail to recognise the difference between describing and explaining. An explanation involves providing detail about what has been described. It requires some comment from candidates on the topic being discussed.

Not including specific religious teachings. In all questions it is vital that reference is made to religious teachings, beliefs and ideas. Without this, it is very difficult to achieve the higher descriptive levels in answers.

Providing generic answers. Many candidates are unsure of specific religious information, so they provide a general answer. It is important that answers reflect specific knowledge and understanding to achieve the higher marks. Religious vocabulary will also help to demonstrate better understanding of religious ideas.

Writing too much or waffling. Waffling in exams is a key mistake. Many candidates write more than the space provided on the examination paper, which means time is wasted that could be given to other questions. Also, mindless waffle that does not answer the question is a waste of valuable examination time.

Only giving *your* opinion on an issue. Evaluation questions clearly state that reference should be made to alternate views. Religious teachings should also be included, and without these it is difficult to achieve the higher-level marks.

What the examiner says

Whatever you may think, examiners are human. And they want you to succeed in Religious Studies. Take a look at the notes below, then, as a starting point to success, familiarise yourself with the topics and key questions covered in the exam.

Note
Exam conditions put us under pressure to remember information and answer questions in a time limit, so it is very easy to make mistakes. Remember, an exam is a test of what you can do, not what you can't do. Examiners are not trying to catch you out or trick you.

Dear Exam Candidate,

I am sure you will want to succeed in your exam. But this does take some preparation and revision. Follow my tips to give yourself a head start.

- Make sure you are clear about which religious tradition you are explaining the ideas for. Many candidates accidentally mix up ideas. (Venn diagrams may help you to compare and contrast ideas.)

- Try to be specific in your answer and give detailed responses. Explain and discuss ideas rather than just present information. (Make a checklist of beliefs and teachings you should try to include.)

- Some of the issues are sensitive or highly controversial. Try to show that you understand this in your answers.

- Make sure you look at and understand how questions are marked. Your responses will be marked according to level descriptors, so you must be careful to ensure you know which questions are AO1 and which are AO2. Look carefully at the number of marks available.

- Attempt as many past paper questions as you can. This will help you to cover several possible question types and will help you to understand how to answer them. Make sure you ask a teacher to mark them or check your answers against the mark scheme.

Good luck!

Examiner

Topics of study

Topic of study	Key questions
1 Relationships What is love? What commitments do we have to others? What responsibilities do we have towards each other? What is the role and purpose of sex? Whose decision is it concerning the use of contraception? Is marriage out of date? How important is the family? Is it necessary to marry in a place of worship? Why do some marriages succeed and others fail? Should people be allowed to remarry? Should it be in a religious building? Should same-sex marriages be allowed in a place of worship?	**3 Looking for meaning** Why do some people believe in God? Why do some people not believe in a God? What is the value of religion in a secular society? How do people experience God? Why do some people use symbols? What influence's people's understanding of God? How do people respond to God? How do religious believers respond to God through vocation? How do religious believers respond to God through worship? How important is worship? How important is a belief in the afterlife? How important are funeral rites?
2 Is it fair? What do we want? Why do people treat others differently? Is equality possible? What should be people's attitudes towards wealth? What do we need? How should we treat others? How does the media influence attitudes? Why are people prejudiced? What is fair? What is unfair?	**4 Our world** How did the universe begin? How can we use our talents? Why should we use our talents? Why are we here? What makes us human? How should we use natural resources? How should animals be treated? Why should we care for the world?

ExamCafé

Let's revise... Relationships

Revision checklist for Topic 1

In order to do well in this topic you will need to:

- [ ] be able to explain religious ideas about love, commitment and responsibilities within relationships – for example, the terms *eros*, *agape*, *philia* and *storge*

- [ ] be able to explain the role and purpose of sex, including reference to pre-marital and extra-marital sex – for example, sex is a gift from God; it is natural and its purpose is procreation

- [ ] be able to discuss the issue of contraception – for example, who should take responsibility in a relationship for contraception and the types that are acceptable

- [ ] assess the value of marriage in today's society – for example, whether marriage is out of date because many couples now cohabit, and the importance of having a family within marriage

- [ ] explain religious beliefs and teachings about the purpose, meaning and nature of marriage, divorce and remarriage – for example, describe a wedding ceremony from different religious traditions and whether same-sex marriages should be allowed in a place of worship

- [ ] explain why different people hold different beliefs and their evidence for their views – for example, why religious believers behave and act in different ways and how their actions are related to their beliefs

- [ ] be able to explain your own views on the issues contained in this topic and support your opinions with relevant evidence – for example, what you think about each of the issues studied and the evidence you can present to support your opinions.

Now it's your turn

You have received lots of advice and tips about revision for this topic. Below are some activities you might like to try.

Activities

1. Make a list of all the key terms you need to know for this topic. Get a friend to test you on them.

2. Make a list of reasons for and against marriage being out of date today.

3. Produce a Venn diagram comparing marriage ceremonies from two different religious traditions.

4. Give two reasons for each of the views below.
   - *Pre-marital sex is always wrong.*
   - *Divorce is too easy.*
   - *Contraception is wrong, as it prevents potential life.*

5. Make a quiz on this topic and give it to a partner, then mark their answers.

6. Produce some revision note cards for this topic. With a partner, test each other on your knowledge of key terms and ideas.

Let's revise... Is it fair?

Revision checklist for Topic 2

In order to do well in this topic you will need to:

- [ ] be able to explain the difference between a want and a need – for example, the things necessary for survival and the things we can live without

- [ ] be able to give examples of how and why people treat others differently, making sure you make reference to the idea of human dignity – for example, ideas about equality, inequality, those things that are fair and unfair

- [ ] be able to explain in detail reasons for and against equality being possible – for example, whether it is ever possible to consider having a society in which everyone is equal and has enough

- [ ] assess people's attitudes towards wealth, how wealth is used and how wealth should be used – for example, why wealth is such an important issue and what can be done to help others

- [ ] explain religious beliefs and teachings about social responsibility and the impact things such as the media have on the world – for example, whose responsibility it is to help others and how the media helps or hinders progress

- [ ] explore issues of justice and equality, looking at why people are prejudiced and why they discriminate, and how others have overcome this and helped those in need – for example, what some individuals and organisations have done to try to promote fairness, justice and equality

- [ ] explain why different people hold different beliefs and the evidence for their views – for example, why religious believers behave and act in different ways and how their actions are related to their beliefs

- [ ] be able to explain your own views on the issues contained in this topic and support your opinions with relevant evidence – for example, what you think about each of the issues studied and the evidence you can present to support your opinions.

Now it's your turn

You have received lots of advice and tips about revision for this topic. Below are some activities you might like to try.

Activities

1 Write down all the key terms for this topic on small pieces of paper. With a partner, pick them at random and test each other on their meaning.

2 Write a quiz on this topic for your class to complete as a test of their knowledge.

3 Give your opinion on the following statements, offering as many reasons as possible for your view.
Wealth should be shared more equally.
All humans are prejudiced in some way.
It is everyone's responsibility to help those in need.

4 Summarise the main religious teachings of this topic in bullet points.

5 Practise some answers to examination questions. Use the levels grid (pages 10–11) to mark your answers, then try to improve them if necessary.

6 Write down ten questions about this topic, then swap with a partner and see if you can answer theirs.

Exam**Café**

Let's revise... Looking for meaning

Revision checklist for Topic 3

In order to do well in this topic you will need to:

☐ be able to explain in detail reasons for and against belief in God – for example, why some people believe in God while others don't

☐ assess the value of religion in today's multicultural society, and state the advantages and disadvantages of religion – for example, whether religion is valuable because it provides community and structure, or whether it actually leads to disputes and separations

☐ be able to explain how different religions view God and how he is represented by them – for example, Christianity understands God through the Trinity, Hinduism through the Trimurti

☐ be able to give examples of how religious believers 'know' God (how he is revealed) and how they respond to him – for example, God may be known through sacred texts and believers may respond to him by dedicating their lives to him by becoming monks or nuns

☐ explain religious beliefs and teachings about death and the afterlife, including the rituals that take place after death and the claim of life after death – for example, Christians have a funeral (with either burial or cremation) and believe in Heaven and Hell, while Hindus only accept cremation and believe in reincarnation

☐ explain why different people hold different beliefs and their evidence for their views – for example, why religious believers behave and act in different ways, and how their actions are related to their beliefs

☐ be able to explain your own views on the issues contained in this topic and support your opinions with relevant evidence – for example, what you think about each of the issues studied and the evidence you can present to support your opinions.

Now it's your turn

You have received lots of advice and tips about revision for this topic. Below are some activities you might like to try.

Activities

1 Write the key terms and definitions on pieces of paper. With a partner see if you can match them up correctly.

2 Produce a concept map showing how different religious traditions view God. Share your ideas with a partner and see if they have the same.

3 Explain two reasons for each statement, making sure you refer to religious teachings.

God must exist – there is so much evidence.
Death rites are very important.
Belief in God is the most important belief for a religious believer.

4 Create a table showing the reasons for and against belief in God. Colour-code your arguments to show how strong they are.

5 Write three examination questions. Then write a mark scheme for each question, using the appropriate levels (see pages 10–11). Swap your questions with a partner and write an answer. Using your mark schemes, mark the answers.

6 Write a speech giving your view about the value of religion in today's society. Then try to give some opposing arguments, referring to religious teachings in your answer.

Let's revise... Our world

Revision checklist for Topic 4

In order to do well in this topic you will need to:

- [ ] be able to explain different views about how the world was created – for example, Christianity and the seven days of creation, and the scientific model of the Big Bang and evolution

- [ ] be able to give examples of how and why religious believers may use their talents for God – for example, how someone may promote religion or sing about their faith

- [ ] be able to explain in detail the place of humankind in the world – for example, why humans are here and what purpose they have

- [ ] explain about issues of stewardship and dominion in terms of how humans use the planet and why the planet should be cared for and not exploited – for example, whether humans are the guardians of the planet or whether it is ours to do with as we please

- [ ] assess the ways in which animals are treated and used – for example, whether animals have rights and whether we should be allowed to use animals for human purposes

- [ ] explain why different people hold different beliefs and their evidence for their views – for example, why religious believers behave and act in different ways, and how their actions are related to their beliefs

- [ ] be able to explain your own views on the issues contained in this topic and support your opinions with relevant evidence – for example, what you think about each of the issues studied, and what evidence you can present to support your opinions.

Now it's your turn

You have received lots of advice and tips about revision for this topic. Below are some activities you might like to try.

Activities

1 Write a key word quiz for a partner to complete.

2 Make a list of the religious and scientific views of creation.

3 Give your opinion on the following statements.
   - *Animals have no rights, so humans can do what they like to them.*
   - *Science explains how the world was created.*
   - *We should look after the world as it is God's creation.*

4 Choose an examination question from this topic and make a checklist of ideas that need to be included in order to get a high-level mark.

5 Make some revision notes for this topic – either concept maps or revision cards.

6 Create a quiz on this topic for a partner to complete and then mark their answers.

Glossary

The list below has all the key terms that occur throughout the WJEC GCSE Religious Studies specification, plus other religious terms used throughout this student book. Spend some time getting to know these words and their definitions. Not only will this aid your understanding of the topic material, but it will also allow you to use the correct terminology and explanations in your GCSE exam.

afterlife continuation of human existence after death

agnostic believing that you cannot know whether or not God exists

akhirah life after death in Islam

anadi Hindu expression for 'beginning-less'

atheistic believing that there is no God

atman the soul in Hinduism, the part of God inside us that moves on to another body or form after death

authority power over others through position or moral teaching

awe sense of wonder in relation to God's creation or presence

Big Bang Theory belief that everything started with a big bang about 14 billion years ago; the universe began to expand, then cooled down, forming the earth and other planets

Buddhist someone who follows Buddhism, a religion based on the teachings of Gautama Buddha

chastity no sex before marriage; remaining sexually pure for marriage

Christian someone who follows Christianity, a religion based on the teachings of Jesus

commitment sense of dedication and obligation to someone or something

community group of people who are joined together because they share something in common

conflict stresses and strains that take place within all human relationships

creation way in which something is uniquely made

discrimination treating groups of people differently or unfairly

dominion being in charge and having power over others

duty a moral or religious obligation

environment surroundings of the place in which human beings live

equality state in which everyone has equal rights

ex nihilo out of nothing

faith belief in God and religious teachings without proof

God ultimate and supreme power to whom worship is given

Hindu someone who follows Hinduism, a religion based on several scriptures

holy days specific days, which vary from religion to religion, when believers put aside time to worship

human dignity treating all human beings with respect regardless of race, sex or social position

human rights rights to the basic things we need in life in order to exist

humanity all the people who live on the earth; a sense of compassion or benevolence towards other members of the human race

identity sense of who you are in terms of attitudes, character and personality

immanence closeness of God and God's involvement with the world and human beings

injustice where everyone is not treated with fairness

Jew someone who follows Judaism, a religion based on the information in the Tenakh

karma the Buddhist belief that a person's deeds affect their past, present and future experiences

literal believing that the Creation account as told in the Bible is true – it happened literally as it is described

love one of the most powerful human emotions that joins people together

miracle unusual, perhaps unbelievable, event that is not easily explained

monotheistic believing in one God

multi-faith drawing on aspects from several different religions

Muslim someone who follows Islam, a religion based on the teachings of Allah (God), as revealed through his prophet, Muhammad

natural resources substances such as oil and coal that occur naturally and have a valuable purpose for humans and the world today

need something that is necessary to survive; without it, we would experience difficulties or hardship

non-literal believing that the creation account as told in the Bible is not a literal account of how creation occurred

non-religious people those who have no religious faith, such as atheists

omnibenevolence all-loving nature of God

omnipotence all-powerful nature of God

omnipresent everywhere at all times, as God is believed to be

omniscience all-knowing nature of God

polytheistic believing in many gods

prayer communication with God, often asking for help or expressing thanks

prejudice judging people to be inferior or superior without cause

reconciliation saying sorry and making up after an argument

reincarnation process whereby the soul moves to another body or form after death

relationship an emotional association between two people

religious believers those who have a faith and belief in a religious system

religious experience experience that is believed to have occurred through contact with God

religious teachings teachings of, for example, Muhammad, Jesus, the Buddha and so on, showing the right way to live life through a particular faith

respect consideration for others; understanding that everyone has value even though their circumstances may be different

responsibilities actions you are expected to carry out

revelation way in which God chooses to reveal God's nature to people

secular non-religious

Sikh someone who follows Sikhism, a religion based originally on the teachings of Guru Nanak and a belief in a universal god

soul part of human nature that is spiritual in form and influences an individual's personality

spiritual not related to material or physical things

stereotype the idea that, if people wear certain types of clothes or drive certain cars, for example, they must all have similar behaviours and values

stewardship God-given responsibility to care for the world

symbolism representation of an idea through actions or images

talent something we are good at

theistic believing there is a God and that God is real

Theory of Evolution argument that life began in simple forms and evolved into the more complex forms of life we see today

tradition belief, custom or common practice

transcendent beyond the physical/natural world; outside human understanding, as God is believed to be

trinity Christian belief that there are three persons within one God: Father, Son and Holy Spirit

universe everything that exists; everything in space and time

vow promise between people, or between a person and God

want something we wish for, but not having it wouldn't bring hardship or poverty

worship form of communication with God; can be practised individually or in a group

Index

Key words from the beginning of each topic are shown in **bold** type, and the page number that is also in bold will take you to a definition of the word.